About Me

BEYOND WORDS
1750 S.W. Skyline Blvd., Suite 20
Portland, Oregon 97221-2543
503-531-8700 / 503-531-8773 fax
www.beyondword.com

First Beyond Words hardcover edition March 2022

This book is for informational purposes only and is not legal advice. The material herein is of general nature only and should not be relied upon in your particular jurisdiction. Please consult a local attorney to assist you with estate planning options, rules and regulations. The use and storage of this book is solely your responsibility. The publishers, author, and all others, are not responsible for any data within this book that is lost, stolen, incomplete or inaccurate. Please consult with counsel to make certain that the the material completed in this book is not contradictory to your legal documents because contradictions can cause delays, confusion, and possibly unintended results. This books is not a substitute for a well-drawn estate plan such as a will or trust.

BEYOND WORDS PUBLISHING and colophon are registered trademarks of Beyond Words Publishing. Beyond Words is an imprint of Simon & Schuster, Inc.

For more information about special discounts for bulk purchases, please contact Beyond Words Special Sales at 503-531-8700 or specialsales@beyondword.com.

Managing Editor: Lindsay S. Easterbrooks-Brown
Editor: Brit Elders
Proofreader: Ashley Van Winkle
Design: Devon Smith/D.Smith Creative, LLC

Manufactured in China

10 9 8 7 6 5 4 3 2 1

Library of Congress Control Number: 2021942100

ISBN: 978-1-58270-864-5

The corporate mission of Beyond Words Publishing, Inc.: *Inspire to Integrity*

About Me

Information You Will Need When I've Passed

Robert E. Kabacy, Esq.

Portland, Oregon

This book is dedicated to my mother who passed away in 2002 following her long battle with cancer. We worked together for several months before her death, organizing her affairs and preparing this book so that handling her estate would be simple, easy, and efficient. She did not want to leave any problems for her family and friends. I hope you find this book useful in easing the difficulties when you lose a loved one.

No matter who you are,
where you came from,
what you achieved, or
how much you're worth...

You are valuable!

Contents

A Note to the Purchaser

If you are buying this book for a loved one, especially an older individual, you might want to offer to help them fill in the information pages. Helping them may be comforting to them and help them avoid feeling overwhelmed. However, some people may not want assistance, which should be respected. This time could also be an opportunity to ask if they have an estate plan in place and to discuss the possibility if they don't.

If you are purchasing this book for yourself, please take the time to write down your wishes and desires. Don't let this book sit on the shelf filled only with good intentions. Whether you are single or have a spouse or life partner, it's an excellent opportunity to consider your estate plan and theirs too.

The passing of a loved one can be very traumatic. This book is designed to organize and simplify the practical wishes of the decedent for their family and friends in a way that can lessen the distress that accompanies death.

Throughout the book you'll see icons to help you navigate. Each main section of the book is denoted by an icon in the margin of the pages. You'll also see a bell icon throughout, drawing your attention to statements of particular import. Here are the icons you will see:

 Section I: My Instructions and Preferences

 Section II: What to Do with My Estate When I'm No Longer Here

 Section III: Probate and Taxes

 Section IV: When Disputes Arise

 Section V: Coping with the Loss of a Loved One

 Resources

 Glossary of Terms

 Notes

 Important information

Acknowledgments

This book was developed over years of practice in the estate planning field, incorporating feedback from clients, personal experience, and the desire to help those in need. Without the constant encouragement of the publishers and editors I could have become easily distracted in the day-to-day tasks at hand, which could have prevented finalizing what you now have in your hands. I am very grateful to my colleagues, clients, friends, and family. A special thank-you goes out to my friends Richard and Michele Cohn. I also want to thank Brit Elders for her insight, guidance, and no-nonsense approach to writing and editing. Finally, I want to thank my wife for her patience, support, and feedback at each step during this journey. I hope that you find this interactive book as valuable as I have when using it at those most difficult times in life.

For the Owner of This Book

It's a simple and very real fact of life that we all pass away. As an estate-planning attorney I have faced this reality with my clients and my family. I've always tried to help my clients prepare for that eventuality but I personally understood the necessity of careful planning when my mother's health deteriorated. She did not want to leave a disorganized mess as a legacy, so we began compiling information that would eventually become the genesis of this book.

When my mother passed, all of the logic, experience, and knowledge that I had accumulated during my professional career was replaced with an enormous flood of emotions and sensory input. Despite the fact that I know intellectually how to deal with this situation, it was extremely comforting to have the exact steps that I needed to take spelled out before me in the book we had created. It was a matter of following directions rather than trying to figure out what to do next. After completing the steps on each page, I experienced a feeling of accomplishment that gave me a sense of control in an environment where I felt I had none. The book that my mother and I had created together, the predecessor to the book in your hands, helped ease the confusion that often accompanies grief when a loved one passes.

By recording vital information in this book, you are planning for future events in a way that will assist your family and friends when you are no longer present to point them in the right direction. They will be able to locate people, assets, documents, logins, and passwords knowing that you have provided them with a sense of clarity. Accessing that type of data is not just helpful, but also comforting because they will be able to make decisions according to your wishes.

The importance of properly closing the affairs of a recently deceased person goes beyond emotional issues. By managing administration correctly, those involved can minimize legal disputes, limit personal liability, and provide an organized system of finalizing details that otherwise may be overlooked. Following appropriate procedures can also prevent legal surprises years later when everyone thought the process had been concluded.

This is *your book*. The title—*About Me*—really is about you. By filling in all relevant information in the initial section you are creating a roadmap for your family, as my mother did for me. Life's path is never a straight line, so please update the information whenever changes occur. Keep your book in a secure location and let your administrator(s) know where they can find it.

Behind the "My Instructions and Preferences" section of the book are several sections that review administration guidelines. They provide valuable tips on estate property, fiduciary responsibility, probate, taxes, grief, resource guides, and a glossary of terms. The material will be beneficial to you and your loved ones, but the first thing you need to begin thinking about is a fiduciary representative for you and your estate. A fiduciary is a person placed in a position of trust.

The person you select as your fiduciary should be someone you trust. They don't have to be related to you; in fact, you might prefer an attorney or other impartial individual to handle the matters of the estate. It should be a person whose values and ethics will guide them as they oversee and administrate your estate. It doesn't matter how large or small your estate is; the person you choose will need to be capable and willing to seek help when necessary.

Your representative should also be a person who will honor the wishes that you outline in this book and in your estate planning documents. It's often a good idea to ask the individual you have in mind if they would be comfortable acting on the behalf of a deceased person and their beneficiaries. You might find that some people are uncomfortable with the responsibilities. In that case, and as a matter of due diligence, it's wise to always have a secondary representative or hire a professional fiduciary.

Most professional fiduciaries charge by the hour. Rates vary, so ask in advance. It is perfectly acceptable to shop for a professional fiduciary and very important that you feel confident in their ability.

Then, if you haven't already prepared estate documents, you should consider this: It is estimated that more than 70 percent of people have done no formal estate planning. Without a written plan, the government, through laws, has dictacted how things will be done at death and who gets your property. The "State" plan usually requires that all estate assets go through the probate court. State laws also require that certain people receive distributions of property in a certain order. Loss of control and loss of value to the estate are just two of the negative consequences of having no formal estate plan.

Take this quick test to see if estate planning is right for you:

1. Are you married?
2. Do you have children?
3. Do you have a preference as to how you should be cared for when you can no longer make decisions (i.e., tube feeding, life support, etc.)?
4. Do you want to designate someone to manage your affairs in the event you are unable to?
5. Do you have life insurance?
6. Do you own your home or other real property?

If you answered "yes" to any of the above questions, some form of estate planning is appropriate for you and can provide significant benefits and peace of mind. If you have done some planning, but it has been a while, it may be time for an update.

Estate planning documents must be tailored to each person's specific needs and desires. Here are some of the more common planning tools:

- Joint ownership
- Wills
- Trusts (revocable, irrevocable, and probate avoidance)
- Family limited partnerships
- Powers of attorney
- Limited liability companies
- Advance directive for healthcare

The type of planning appropriate for you depends on your particular circumstances. However, there are common goals of estate planning that apply no matter which type of documents you use. These are some of the common goals of estate planning in order of priority:

- Take care of you during your lifetime
- Provide for incapacity

- Develop a distribution plan
- Avoid probate
- Reduce or eliminate taxes

An estate plan should be updated in any of these events:

- After divorce
- After the birth of a child
- After the death of a relative named in the plan
- After receipt of inheritance or other windfall
- After a change in intent
- After a change in the tax laws
- After moving to another state
- After marriage
- Or as a general rule, about every three years

Remember that estate planning does not have to be complicated or expensive. It is also not reserved for those who make a lot of money. Estate planning is for people who want to let others know what to do in the event of incapacity or death, to make the administration process easier, and to reduce taxes where possible.

Once you have completed the "My Instructions and Preferences" section of this book and settled on a fiduciary, you might want to have a conversation with or write a letter to your chosen personal representative to tell them where they can locate this book and how to access it, as it should be kept in a secure location, such as a safe. Mail the letter to the fiduciary or give it to an attorney to be delivered to the fiduciary when you have passed. You will rest easier in the knowledge that your wishes will be known.

A sample letter is on the following page.

A Sample Letter

This letter is only an example of what you might choose to write:

Date: ______________________

Dear ______________________,

I would like for you to be my fiduciary or personal representative when I pass or if I am incapacitated because I have come to appreciate your decisions in life. I trust that you will oversee my estate and my preferences with the ethical and moral values and the compassion that you employ daily.

I realize that this is a tremendous responsibility and that I may be asking a lot of you but I want to make my death or incapacity easier on you and everyone associated with me. I think you can help me achieve that.

I have completed a book called *About Me* that is filled with information that should help you understand my estate and know my wishes. The book is located at: ____________________
____.

To access the book, which has been secured at (*suggested locations: safe, safety-deposit box, attorney's office*) ____,
you will need the (*suggestions: key, combination, attorney's name and number*), which is ______
____.

Thank you for being there for me.

With appreciation and respect,

Signature: ____________________________________

About Me

For My Loved Ones

In this book I have shared personal details and specific choices that I would like you to make on my behalf. The information represents or is connected to me and can be used in the event of my incapacity or after my death. While this is not a substitute for legal documents or legal advice, it can help you by clearly stating my wishes and providing general information that can help you navigate the processes when I cannot act for myself.

This book is not meant to be a comprehensive resource for all aspects of administration of my property but rather a depot of data and guidance to get you started when I can't be there for you. I realize that you may be feeling many emotions and my hope is that this book will ease some of the burden you may feel after my incapacity and certainly after I've passed.

Section I

My Instructions and Preferences

Please maintain this book in a secure location.

Place a note (sample below) in your wallet or purse, on the refrigerator, or in another highly visible place with the location of this book or the contact information of the person (professional, family member, or trusted friend) who has it. Suggested secure locations: safety-deposit box, home safe, or other secure location within your home.

A Sample Note

Upon my incapacity or passing, to locate important information about me call (name)______________________ at (phone number)______________________ or look in this secure location:____.

Upon My Passing

Call (name): ______________________________

Relationship: ______________________________

Phone: ______________________________

Alternate phone: ______________________________

This person may be able to assist you and be supportive in the following days.

The person listed above may be a family member, friend, pastor, priest, rabbi, counselor, or other person who has had experience addressing the emotional issues surrounding death.

Summary of Immediate Steps in the Event of Death

Contact the funeral home/mortuary (if necessary) ______________________________

at ______________________________.

Contact my family and friends. A phone/text/email tree works well and you can expect to receive tremendous compassion and support from most. Some people may not know what to say, but they will certainly mean well.

Locate estate planning and legal documents. They may be at home or with my attorney. This book should help you identify where I have secured important documents.

Please identify and notify my chosen fiduciary, who should take responsibility for administration of my estate. Please read the section of this book on Fiduciary Responsibilities and share it with my chosen fiduciary. It will help all involved better understand what needs to be done in the coming weeks.

Please do not remove items from my residence as they are part of my estate and need to be inventoried.

Call Social Security and notify that agency of my death: 1-800-722-1213.

Request death certificates. This can often be done through the mortuary. You will receive one registered copy from the state and will need six to ten additional copies.

Follow the guidance I have provided in this book. Please note that I have left areas blank that don't apply to me or for which I have no preference.

Instructions Depending on Where I Pass

If I am in the hospital or in hospice:

Ask the hospital staff to call the mortuary. The name of the mortuary, contact, and number is:

____

____

If I was home and under hospice care:
Call (hospice service, contact person, and phone number):

____

____

If I was at home and not under hospice care:

Call 911. Tell the dispatcher that I died at home. An officer will be dispatched. Tell the officer the following:

1. My cause of death (if known)
2. My medications (see my medications list on page 17)

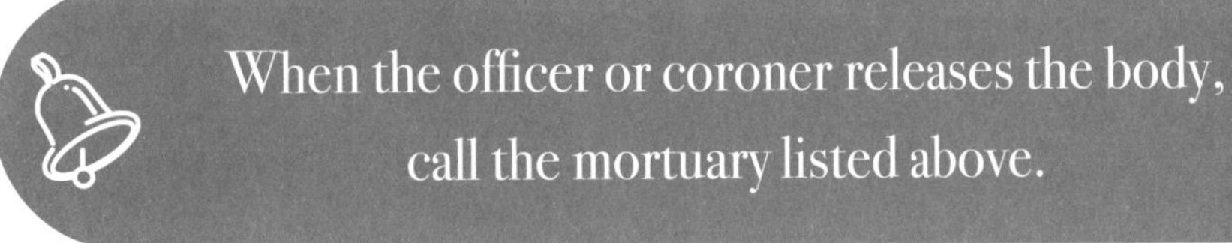

When the officer or coroner releases the body,
call the mortuary listed above.

Organ Donations

Consult with local counsel for state or local rules as these pages are not a substitute for legal documents.

_____ I want all usable organs donated.

_____ I want select organs to be donated (see next page).

_____ I do not want my organs donated.

______________________________ ______________________________

Signature Date

If my organs are to be donated, you must make arrangements with my doctor or the hospital immediately. Organs can begin to deteriorate within twelve hours. Please notify those responsible for the disposition of my body of my wishes. Many states allow for designation of organ donorship on a driver's license. If I have a driver's license, please check it.

Donating Organs (Sample Uniform Donor Card)

I, ______________________________, have spoken to my family about organ and tissue donation. The people listed here have witnessed my commitment to be a donor.

CIRCLE THE ORGANS AND/OR TISSUE THAT YOU WISH TO DONATE:

Skin	Vascular tissue	Kidneys
Eyes	Heart and heart valves	Bone
Liver	Tendon	Pancreas
Cartilage and fascia	Lungs	Other

I wish to (select one)

_____ Donate my entire body for medical education. (Additional forms may be required.)
_____ Donate any organs and tissues.
_____ Donate only the organs or tissues circled above.

______________________________ ______________________

Signature of Donor Date

______________________________ ______________________

Signature of Witness 1 Date

______________________________ ______________________

Signature of Witness 2 Date

My Personal Information

My full legal name is: ______________________________

I am also known as: ______________________________

Maiden name: ______________________________

My date of birth is: ______________________________

Place of birth is: ______________________________

My Social Security number is: ______________________________

My address is: ______________________________

____

My mailing address is: ______________________________

____

My telephone number is: ______________________________

My cell number is: ______________________________

My additional phone numbers: ______________________________

My marital status: ____________________ Date of marriage: ____________________

The name of my spouse/partner is: ____

Phone: ____________________________

My children (circle A for Alive or D for Deceased) are:

Name: ____ A D

Date of birth: ____________________ Date of death: ____________________

Phone: ____________________________

Name: ____ A D

Date of birth: ____________________ Date of death: ____________________

Phone: ____________________________

Name: ____ A D

Date of birth: ____________________ Date of death: ____________________

Phone: ____________________________

My Personal Information, cont.

My children, (circle A for Alive or D for Deceased) are, cont.

Name: ______________________________ A D

Date of birth: ______________ Date of death: ______________

Phone: ______________

Name: ______________________________ A D

Date of birth: ______________ Date of death: ______________

Phone: ______________

Use the Notes pages at the back of *About Me* as necessary.

My grandchildren (circle A for Alive or D for Deceased) are:

Name: ______________________________ A D

Date of birth: ______________ Date of death: ______________

Phone: ______________

Name: ______________________________ A D

Date of birth: ______________ Date of death: ______________

Phone: ______________

Name: ______________________________ A D

Date of birth: ______________ Date of death: ______________

Phone: ______________

Name: ______________________________ A D

Date of birth: ______________ Date of death: ______________

Phone: ______________

Name: ______________________________ A D

Date of birth: ______________ Date of death: ______________

Phone: ______________

Name: ______________________________ A D

Date of birth: ______________ Date of death: ______________

Phone: ______________

My Personal Information, cont.

My grandchildren (circle A for Alive or D for Deceased) are, cont.

Name: ______________________________ A D

Date of birth: ______________ Date of death: ______________

Phone: ______________

Name: ______________________________ A D

Date of birth: ______________ Date of death: ______________

Phone: ______________

Name: ______________________________ A D

Date of birth: ______________ Date of death: ______________

Phone: ______________

Name: ______________________________ A D

Date of birth: ______________ Date of death: ______________

Phone: ______________

My parents and/or stepparents (circle A for Alive or D for Deceased) are:

Name: ____ A D

Date of birth: ____________________ Date of death: ____________________

Phone: ________________________

Name: ____ A D

Date of birth: ____________________ Date of death: ____________________

Phone: ________________________

Name: ____ A D

Date of birth: ____________________ Date of death: ____________________

Phone: ________________________

Name: ____ A D

Date of birth: ____________________ Date of death: ____________________

Phone: ________________________

My Personal Information, cont.

My previous spouse(s) or partner(s) (circle A for Alive or D for Deceased) are:

Name: ______________________________ A D

Date of marriage: ______________ Date of dissolution: ______________

Date of birth: ______________ Date of death: ______________

Phone: ______________

Name: ______________________________ A D

Date of marriage: ______________ Date of dissolution: ______________

Date of birth: ______________ Date of death: ______________

Phone: ______________

Use the Notes pages at the back of *About Me* as necessary.

My occupation is: ____

I am: ___ actively employed ___ self-employed ___ retired

My employer is: ____

Phone: ______________________

Benefits that my employer offers are: ______________________________

____

My religious preference is: ____________________________________

My place of worship is: ______________________________________

Phone: ______________________

My military service includes: ___________________________________

My affiliations and memberships include: ____________________________

____

____

Additional Information about Me

I am a citizen of: ____

_____ I have a passport. The number is: ______________________________
It is located: ____

_____ I have a driver's license. The number is: _________________________
It is located: ____

_____ I have an ID card. The number is: ______________________________
It is located: ____

_____ I am a veteran. My veteran ID is:______________________________
It is located: ____

_____ I own a firearm(s). The permit number(s): _______________________
The permit(s) can be located at: _________________________________
The firearm(s) can be located at: _________________________________
____

_____ The firearms are federally registered. Please take appropriate steps with local, state, and/or federal authorities.

_____ I have a gun trust.

My Current Medications

Example:

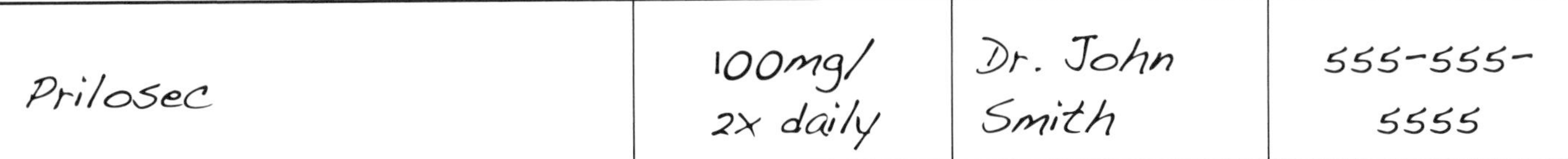

Prilosec	100mg/ 2x daily	Dr. John Smith	555-555-5555

Name of Drug	Dosage	Prescribing Physician	Phone Number

My Current Medications, cont.

Name of Drug	Dosage	Prescribing Physician	Phone Number

My Current Medications, cont.

Name of Drug	Dosage	Prescribing Physician	Phone Number

Family and Friends to Contact

Connect with family and friends; they'll be there for emotional support. Set up a network, like a telephone or email tree, so that no one person is tasked with all of the communication. This also helps ensure that no one is overlooked. I have listed the key people I would like to have notified. Be sensitive and conscious of the grief everyone is feeling and try to be emotionally supportive whenever possible. As you connect with others, keep a few things in mind:

Every person grieves differently. There is not one right way to cope with the loss of a loved one.

Some people may need to speak to someone they are comfortable with like a close friend, others may seek the guidance of a clergyman, and some may need to seek the assistance of a counselor.

If a family member or friend is unable to cope with the loss and suffering physically and/or emotionally, you may need to contact their family physician or therapist to seek guidance. In any case, be cautious about intervening because everyone will react in their own private way.

When you speak with others, encourage comforting memories.
Sharing stories and recollections of happier times helps to ease emotional pain.

Please Notify the Following People

These people were important to me. Please let them know of my passing and ask them to share with others that may have known me.

Name: ______________________________

Relationship: ______________________ Phone: ______________________

Name: ______________________________

Relationship: ______________________ Phone: ______________________

Name: ______________________________

Relationship: ______________________ Phone: ______________________

Name: ______________________________

Relationship: ______________________ Phone: ______________________

Name: ______________________________

Relationship: ______________________ Phone: ______________________

Name: ______________________________

Relationship: ______________________ Phone: ______________________

Family and Friends to Contact, cont.

Name: ____________________

Relationship: ____________ Phone: ____________

Name: ____________________

Relationship: ____________ Phone: ____________

Name: ____________________

Relationship: ____________ Phone: ____________

Name: ____________________

Relationship: ____________ Phone: ____________

Name: ____________________

Relationship: ____________ Phone: ____________

Name: ____________________

Relationship: ____________ Phone: ____________

Name: ____________________

Relationship: ____________ Phone: ____________

Funeral Arrangements

After my death my body is to be taken to (name of mortuary or other facility):

____

Contact person: ______________________ Phone: ______________________

Call the mortuary—day or night—and they will pick up my body. Should you reach the facility's answering service, they will notify the appropriate personnel.

Please notify my place of worship: ______________________________

____

Disposition of my remains shall be stated in my estate planning documents. If I have not completed the documents, I wish to be (cremated, buried, other): ______________________ (see also page 29).

_____ I have prepaid for my cremation or burial.
_____ I have not prepaid for my cremation or burial.

If I have prepaid for the disposition of my remains, receipts and paperwork can be found in the folder at the back of this book or at this location: ______________________

____

_____ I have prearranged services at a funeral home or other location.
_____ I have not prearranged services at a funeral home or other location.

Funeral Arrangements, cont.

If I have made arrangements for services, the receipts and paperwork can be found in the folder at the back of this book or at this location:

____

____

____

____

____

Many states have legal requirements for giving instructions in this regard. The above may not comply with such legal requirements. Please consult a local attorney for assistance.

I would prefer to have:

_____ A funeral and graveside service
_____ A memorial service or celebration of my life
_____ Both a funeral and a memorial or celebration of life service
_____ I prefer not to have a funeral or memorial service or celebration of my life

If I have opted to have a funeral, I nominate the following person(s) to coordinate and arrange the event:

Funeral planner: ____

Relationship: ____________________________ Phone: ____________________________

Back-up funeral planner: ____

Relationship: ____________________________ Phone: ____________________________

_____ I have specific wishes outlined on the following page.
_____ I do not have specific wishes for my funeral/celebration of life, in which case my funeral planner(s) may take care of whatever reasonable arrangements they determine.

My Funeral

PLEASE CHECK ALL THAT APPLY:

I request:

_____ An open casket
_____ A closed casket
_____ A presentation of the urn
_____ I have selected a picture of me to be displayed during the service and/or memorial. It can be located ______________________________

_____ I request the following music or song(s) be included in the program at appropriate times:

Title: ____________________ Artist: ____________________

Title: ____________________ Artist: ____________________

Title: ____________________ Artist: ____________________

Title: ____________________ Artist: ____________________

Title: ____________________ Artist: ____________________

Title: ____________________ Artist: ____________________

Title: ____________________ Artist: ____________________

I request the following in regard to flowers at the funeral and/or memorial service:

_____ Flowers at the funeral and/or memorial service. My favorite flowers are: ___________

____

_____ A memorial contribution in lieu of flowers to charities (see page 30).

I request the following in regard to readings at my funeral and/or memorial service:

_____ The following readings should be read at my service: ______________________

____

____

____

____

____

_____ My family and funeral planner should select appropriate readings based on their knowledge of me.

My Funeral, cont.

_____ I request the following people be permitted to speak at my service:

Name: ______________________________ Phone: ______________________________

Name: ______________________________ Phone: ______________________________

Name: ______________________________ Phone: ______________________________

Name: ______________________________ Phone: ______________________________

_____ I prefer the following people not speak at my service:

____

____

_____ I would like a reception after the service as a celebration of my life to be held at:

____

I would like $______ set aside from my estate for my funeral and reception. It should be made available to my fiduciary and can be obtained from the following bank account:____________

____

Disposition of Remains

_____ If I have chosen to be buried, I would like to be interred at (cemetery):

____

_____ If I have chosen to be cremated, I would like my ashes to be disposed of in the following way:

My ashes are to be interred at ______________________________

My ashes are to be ______________________________

I hereby certify that the above requests are my wishes. (These wishes may not be followed if not signed and witnessed by two witnesses.)

______________________________ ______________________________
Signature Date

______________________________ ______________________________
Signature of Witness 1 Date

______________________________ ______________________________
Signature of Witness 2 Date

My Memorial Directive

In lieu of flowers at my funeral or memorial service, I would like all memorials or remembrances in my name be used for the benefit of:

____

____

Through the following organization:

Organization name: ______________________________

Address: ____________________________________

____

Contact person: ________________ Phone: ________________

Contributions should be sent to the above organization with a note indicating such contribution is in my name and for the benefit of the above listed organization.

Contributions to the above organization may be tax deductible for the donor. Contact the organization and your tax advisor to discuss available deductions.

Please share my preference for contributions in the following way (check all that apply):

_____ Notify those attending my funeral or memorial service.
_____ Inform my family and friends.
_____ Attach it to my will and give it to my heirs and beneficiaries.
_____ Publish it a local paper of general circulation or in an online notice.
_____ Other: ____

____

______________________________ ______________________________
Signature Date

My Obituary and Headstone

I would like the following included in any obituary or on any headstone. Please provide it to the funeral home director and make arrangements for its publication in the following newspaper and/or online resource:

____

____

If I've left the following section blank, then it is up to my representatives to write my obituary.

Details for My Obituary

____

____

____

____

____

____

____

Details for My Headstone

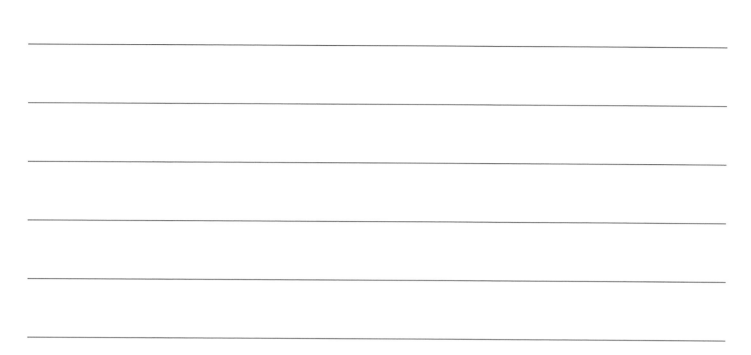

This information should be provided to the funeral home or company making the marker.

Notify My Primary Physician

Name: ______________________________

Clinic name: ______________________________

Address: ______________________________

____

Phone: ____________________ My blood type is: ____________________

Please notify my physician of my passing during regular business hours.

My Professional Advisors

List additional professional advisors in the Notes pages in the back of this book.

Please contact the following professionals if I am incapacitated or deceased.

Additional Doctors Who Have Treated Me

Doctor: ______________________ Specialty: ______________________

Address: ____

____

Phone: ______________________

Doctor: ______________________ Specialty: ______________________

Address: ____

____

Phone: ______________________

Doctor: ______________________ Specialty: ______________________

Address: ____

____

Phone: ______________________

My Professional Advisors, cont.

Additional Doctors Who Have Treated Me, cont.

Doctor: ______________________ Specialty: ______________________
Address: ____
____
Phone: ______________________

Doctor: ______________________ Specialty: ______________________
Address: ____
____
Phone: ______________________

Doctor: ______________________ Specialty: ______________________
Address: ____
____
Phone: ______________________

Doctor: ______________________ Specialty: ______________________
Address: ____
____
Phone: ______________________

Lawyers

My primary attorney is: ______________________________

Address: ______________________________

____

Phone: ____________________

My additional attorney is: ______________________________

Address: ______________________________

____

Phone: ____________________

Accountants

My accountant is: ______________________________

Address: ______________________________

____

Phone: ____________________

My tax preparer is: ______________________________

Address: ______________________________

____

Phone: ____________________

My Professional Advisors, cont.

Financial Planner

My financial planner is: ______________________________

Address: ______________________________

____

Phone: ____________________

Banker

My banker is: ______________________________

Address: ______________________________

____

Phone: ____________________

Insurance Agent

My insurance agent is: ______________________________

Address: ______________________________

____

Phone: ____________________

My additional insurance agent is: ______________________________

Address: ______________________________

____

Phone: ____________________

See page 41 for more information abot insurance providers.

Additional Advisors

Advisor: ______________________ Role: ______________________
Address: ____
____
Phone: ______________________

Advisor: ______________________ Role: ______________________
Address: ____
____
Phone: ______________________

Advisor: ______________________ Role: ______________________
Address: ____
____
Phone: ______________________

Advisor: ______________________ Role: ______________________
Address: ____
____
Phone: ______________________

Advisor: ______________________ Role: ______________________
Address: ____
____
Phone: ______________________

Location of Estate Planning Documents

Letter of last instruction for disposition of personal effects is located: ____________________

____

Will/trust is located: ____

Power of attorney documents are located: __________________________

Medical power of attorney is located: _____________________________

DNR (do not resuscitate) is located: ______________________________

See page 29 for disposition of remains.

Notes: ____

____

____

____

____

____

Location of Additional Vital Documents

My Social Security number is: ______________________________

My Social Security card is located: ______________________________

Birth certificate(s) are located: ______________________________

Marriage certificate(s) are located: ______________________________

Divorce or dissolution paperwork is located: ______________________________

My post office box is located: ______________________________

The key is located: ______________________________

The combination is: ______________________________

Insurance Policies

Life insurance provider: ______________________________

Policy amount: ______________________________

Agent: ____________________ Phone: ____________________

Policy number: ____________________ Located: ____________________

Life insurance provider: ______________________________

Policy amount: ______________________________

Agent: ____________________ Phone: ____________________

Policy number: ____________________ Located: ____________________

Health insurance provider: ______________________________

Agent: ____________________ Phone: ____________________

Policy number: ____________________ Located: ____________________

Location of Additional Vital Documents, cont.

Dental insurance provider: ______________________________

Agent: ______________________ Phone: ______________________

Policy number: ______________________ Located: ______________________

Vision insurance provider: ______________________________

Agent: ______________________ Phone: ______________________

Policy number: ______________________ Located: ______________________

Disability insurance provider: ______________________________

Agent: ______________________ Phone: ______________________

Policy number: ______________________ Located: ______________________

Accident insurance provider: ______________________________

Agent: ______________________ Phone: ______________________

Policy number: ______________________ Located: ______________________

Auto insurance provider: ______________________________

Agent: ______________________ Phone: ______________________

Policy number: ______________________ Located: ______________________

Auto insurance provider: ______________________________

Agent: ______________________ Phone: ______________________

Policy number: ______________________ Located: ______________________

Home/rental insurance provider: ______________________________

Home/rental address: ______________________________

____

Agent: ______________ Phone: ______________

Policy number: ______________ Located: ______________

Home/rental insurance provider: ______________________________

Home/rental address: ______________________________

____

Agent: ______________ Phone: ______________

Policy number: ______________ Located: ______________

Umbrella insurance provider: ______________________________

Policy amount: ______________________________

Agent: ______________ Phone: ______________

Policy number: ______________ Located: ______________

<u>Other insurance may include VA, intensive care, extended care, ambulance insurance, medevac, and so forth.</u>

Type: ______________________________

Agent: ______________ Phone: ______________

Policy number: ______________ Located: ______________

Type: ______________________________

Agent: ______________ Phone: ______________

Policy number: ______________ Located: ______________

Location of Deeds and Titles

Real estate deed 1 is located: ______________________________

Approximate real estate value: ______________________________

Mortgage holder: ____________________ Phone: ____________________

Location of property: ______________________________

____

Real estate deed 2 is located: ______________________________

Approximate real estate value: ______________________________

Mortgage holder: ____________________ Phone: ____________________

Location of property: ______________________________

____

Real estate deed 3 is located: ______________________________

Approximate real estate value: ______________________________

Mortgage holder: ____________________ Phone: ____________________

Location of property: ______________________________

____

> Additional deeds can be listed in the Notes pages in the back of this book.

Notes: ______________________________

____

Vehicles

> Please use pencil or additional Notes pages located in the back of this book, so that you can change information if you sell or purchase other vehicles.

Vehicle title is located: ______________________________
VIN: ______________________________
Make: ______________ Model: ______________ Year: ________

Vehicle title is located: ______________________________
VIN: ______________________________
Make: ______________ Model: ______________ Year: ________

Vehicle title is located: ______________________________
VIN: ______________________________
Make: ______________ Model: ______________ Year: ________

Vehicle title is located: ______________________________
VIN: ______________________________
Make: ______________ Model: ______________ Year: ________

Vehicle title is located: ______________________________
VIN: ______________________________
Make: ______________ Model: ______________ Year: ________

Vehicle title is located: ______________________________
VIN: ______________________________
Make: ______________ Model: ______________ Year: ________

Location of Deeds and Titles, cont.

ATV title is located: ____________________

VIN: ____________________

Make: ____________ Model: ____________ Year: ________

RV title is located: ____________________

VIN: ____________________

Make: ____________ Model: ____________ Year: ________

Boat title is located: ____________________

VIN: ____________________

Make: ____________ Model: ____________ Year: ________

Notes: ____________________

Tax and Investment Records

Tax Record Location

Last year's tax records: ______________________________

____

Last 7 years tax records: ______________________________

____

Foreign tax records: ______________________________

____

Other tax records: ______________________________

____

Investment Documents Location

Financial documents are located: ______________________________

Investment bank records are located: ______________________________

Bank: ____________________ Account number: ____________________

Investment bank records are located: ______________________________

Bank: ____________________ Account number: ____________________

Investment bank records are located: ______________________________

Bank: ____________________ Account number: ____________________

Tax and Investment Records, cont.

Stock Certificates

1. ____________________
2. ____________________
3. ____________________
4. ____________________
5. ____________________
6. ____________________
7. ____________________
8. ____________________
9. ____________________
10. ____________________

Brokerage Firm(s) (If Used)

____

____

Bonds

1. ____________________
2. ____________________
3. ____________________
4. ____________________
5. ____________________

Mutual Funds

1. ____________________
2. ____________________
3. ____________________
4. ____________________
5. ____________________

Annuities

1. ____________________
2. ____________________
3. ____________________
4. ____________________
5. ____________________

Precious Metals and Other Investments

DESCRIPTION AND LOCATION

1. ____________________
2. ____________________
3. ____________________
4. ____________________
5. ____________________

Tax and Investment Records, cont.

Retirement Plans

401(k): ____________________

Traditional IRA: ____________________

Roth IRA: ____________________

SEP IRA: ____________________

Simple IRA: ____________________

Other plans (such as 403(b), 457(b), HSA): ____________________

____

____

Notes: ____________________

____

____

____

Bank and Currency Accounts

The documents are located: ______________________________

Checking account bank: ______________________________
Phone: ______________________________
Account number: ______________________________
Branch address: ______________________________
____

Checking account bank: ______________________________
Phone: ______________________________
Account number: ______________________________
Branch address: ______________________________
____

Savings account bank: ______________________________
Phone: ______________________________
Account number: ______________________________
Branch address: ______________________________
____

Savings account bank: ______________________________
Phone: ______________________________
Account number: ______________________________
Branch address: ______________________________
____

Bank and Currency Accounts, cont.

Certificates of Deposit

Bank: ______________________________

Phone: ______________________________

Account number: ______________________________

Branch address: ______________________________

____

Bank: ______________________________

Phone: ______________________________

Account number: ______________________________

Branch address: ______________________________

____

Treasury Bills

Bank: ______________________________

Phone: ______________________________

Account number: ______________________________

Branch address: ______________________________

____

Bank: ______________________________

Phone: ______________________________

Account number: ______________________________

Branch address: ______________________________

____

Savings Bonds

Issue date: ______________________ Print date: ______________________

Serial number: ____

Issue date: ______________________ Print date: ______________________

Serial number: ____

Issue date: ______________________ Print date: ______________________

Serial number: ____

Cryptocurrency

Type (Bitcoin/Crypto/digital currency): ______________________

Certificate identification number: ______________________

Web address: ____

Private key: ____

Non-Fungible Tokens (NFTs)

Type: ____

Location: ____

Access key: ____

List additional currency accounts in the Notes pages in the back of this book.

Outstanding Loans

These documents are located: ____

____

Lien holders: ____

____

Mortgage holder: ____
Account number: ____

Mortgage holder: ____
Account number: ____

Vehicles

See page 45 for vehicle details.

1. Make: ______________________ Model: ______________ Year: ________

   Lien holder: ____

   Account number: ____

Vehicles, cont.

2. Make: ______________________ Model: ______________ Year: _______

Lien holder: ____

Account number: ____

3. Make: ______________________ Model: ______________ Year: _______

Lien holder: ____

Account number: ____

4. Make: ______________________ Model: ______________ Year: _______

Lien holder: ____

Account number: ____

5. Make: ______________________ Model: ______________ Year: _______

Lien holder: ____

Account number: ____

List additional vehicles or changes in the Notes pages at the back of this book.

Outstanding Loans, cont.

Student Loans

Lender: ____________________

Account number: ____________________

Line of Credit

Lender: ____________________

Account number: ____________________

Personal Loan

Lender: ____________________

Account number: ____________________

Other Loans (Including Personal Business Loans)

Lender: ____________________

Account number: ____________________

Other Loans (Including Personal Business Loans), cont.

Lender: ______________________________

Account number: ______________________________

Lender: ______________________________

Account number: ______________________________

Lender: ______________________________

Account number: ______________________________

Lender: ______________________________

Account number: ______________________________

Lender: ______________________________

Account number: ______________________________

Notes: ______________________________

____

____

Credit/Debit Cards

Issuer: ______________________________

Debit/credit account number: ______________________________

Name on card: ______________________________

Issuer: ______________________________

Debit/credit account number: ______________________________

Name on card: ______________________________

Issuer: ______________________________

Debit/credit account number: ______________________________

Name on card: ______________________________

Issuer: ______________________________

Debit/credit account number: ______________________________

Name on card: ______________________________

Issuer: ______________________________

Debit/credit account number: ______________________________

Name on card: ______________________________

Issuer: ______________________________

Debit/credit account number: ______________________________

Name on card: ______________________________

Issuer: ______________________________

Debit/credit account number: ______________________________

Name on card: ______________________________

Retail Cards (Department Store, Hardware Store, etc.)

Issuer: ______________________________
Account number: ______________________________
Name on card: ______________________________

Issuer: ______________________________
Account number: ______________________________
Name on card: ______________________________

Issuer: ______________________________
Account number: ______________________________
Name on card: ______________________________

Issuer: ______________________________
Account number: ______________________________
Name on card: ______________________________

Issuer: ______________________________
Account number: ______________________________
Name on card: ______________________________

Issuer: ______________________________
Account number: ______________________________
Name on card: ______________________________

Issuer: ______________________________
Account number: ______________________________
Name on card: ______________________________

Credit/Debit Cards, cont.

Gas Cards

Issuer: ______________________________

Account number: ______________________________

Name on card: ______________________________

Issuer: ______________________________

Account number: ______________________________

Name on card: ______________________________

Issuer: ______________________________

Account number: ______________________________

Name on card: ______________________________

Other Personal Cards

Issuer: ______________________________

Account number: ______________________________

Name on card: ______________________________

Issuer: ______________________________

Account number: ______________________________

Name on card: ______________________________

Credit Cards Used for Business

Issuer: ______________________________

Account number: ______________________________

Name on card: ______________________________

Issuer: ______________________________

Account number: ______________________________

Name on card: ______________________________

Issuer: ______________________________

Account number: ______________________________

Name on card: ______________________________

Issuer: ______________________________

Account number: ______________________________

Name on card: ______________________________

Issuer: ______________________________

Account number: ______________________________

Name on card: ______________________________

Please cancel all of my credit/debit cards as soon as possible.

Security, Safes, and Safety-Deposit Boxes

Home Security System

My home security company is: ______________________________

Account number: ____________________ Phone: ____________________

The security code for my home is: ______________________________

Safety-Deposit Box(es)

Bank: ______________________________

Box number: ______________________________

Key location (optional): ______________________________

Bank: ______________________________

Box number: ______________________________

Key location (optional): ______________________________

Bank: ______________________________

Box number: ______________________________

Key location (optional): ______________________________

_____ The keys for the safety-deposit box are located: ______________________

_____ My personal representative has been told where the keys are.

Safes

Location and description of safe: ____________________

____

The combination, key, or access card is located at: ____________________

Location and description of safe: ____________________

____

The combination, key, or access card is located at: ____________________

I have a gun safe located at: ____________________

____

The combination, key, or access card is located at: ____________________

Notes: ____________________

____

____

____

____

____

____

My E-Universe

Our digital world is growing daily and many of us keep up with technology that seems to change from moment to moment. Some of us are using optical scans, facial recognition, and fingerprint technologies to open devices, including safes, smartphones, and other digital equipment. I recommend that you always have a password or code as a backup entry, as there may be a time when a fingerprint or optical scan or facial recognition is not possible.

Computers

My home computer login is: ______________________________

The password is: ______________________________

My laptop computer login is: ______________________________

The password is: ______________________________

Cellular Phones

Model: ____________________ Passcode: ____________________

Model: ____________________ Passcode: ____________________

Model: ____________________ Passcode: ____________________

Other Devices (iPads, Kindles, etc.)

Model: ______________________ Passcode: ______________________

Model: ______________________ Passcode: ______________________

Model: ______________________ Passcode: ______________________

Model: ______________________ Passcode: ______________________

Software (Subscription-Based, etc.)

1. ______________________ Password: ______________________
2. ______________________ Password: ______________________
3. ______________________ Password: ______________________
4. ______________________ Password: ______________________
5. ______________________ Password: ______________________
6. ______________________ Password: ______________________
7. ______________________ Password: ______________________
8. ______________________ Password: ______________________
9. ______________________ Password: ______________________
10. ______________________ Password: ______________________

Email

Service provider: ____

Account: ______________________ Password: ______________________

Email continued on the next page

My E-Universe, cont.

Email, cont.

Service provider: ____________________

Account: ____________________ Password: ____________________

Service provider: ____________________

Account: ____________________ Password: ____________________

I have a password vault or manager that can be accessed on:

____

____

Website

My website address is: ____________________

Account name: ____________________ Password: ____________________

Host: ____________________ Phone: ____________________

Social Media

Social media site: ____________________

User ID: ____________________ Password: ____________________

Social Media, cont.

Social media site: ______________________________
User ID: ______________________ Password: ______________________

Social media site: ______________________________
User ID: ______________________ Password: ______________________

Social media site: ______________________________
User ID: ______________________ Password: ______________________

Social media site: ______________________________
User ID: ______________________ Password: ______________________

Social media site: ______________________________
User ID: ______________________ Password: ______________________

Additional Online Accounts

Amazon: ______________________ Password: ______________________
Android: ______________________ Password: ______________________
Apple: ______________________ Password: ______________________
Microsoft: ______________________ Password: ______________________

Additional: ______________________________

____

____

My E-Universe, cont.

Virtual Wallet

Type: ______________________________

Virtual wallet: ____________________ Password: ____________________

Type: ______________________________

Virtual wallet: ____________________ Password: ____________________

See page 53 for crypocurrency.

Other (Utilities, Entertainment, etc.)

Account: ____________________ Password: ____________________

Account: ____________________ Password: ____________________

Account: ____________________ Password: ____________________

Account: ____________________ Password: ____________________

Account: ____________________ Password: ____________________

Account: ____________________ Password: ____________________

Account: ____________________ Password: ____________________

Account: ____________________ Password: ____________________

Please change my digital access passwords to these accounts and close each account when it is no longer necessary.

Pets and Animals

At this time I have the following pets. Some may require specific care—such as medications, diet, and exercise—or have a medical history, which I've listed under special instructions.

Type of pet: ______________________ Name: ______________________
Microchip information and special instructions: ______________________
____

Type of pet: ______________________ Name: ______________________
Microchip information and special instructions: ______________________
____

Type of pet: ______________________ Name: ______________________
Microchip information and special instructions: ______________________
____

Type of pet: ______________________ Name: ______________________
Microchip information and special instructions: ______________________
____

Type of pet: ______________________ Name: ______________________
Microchip information and special instructions: ______________________
____

Type of pet: ______________________ Name: ______________________
Microchip information and special instructions: ______________________
____

Pets and Animals, cont.

I would like ______________________________

to care for my pets if they are willing. If they are unable or do not wish to care for my pets, I would like ______________________________

to care for them.

If both parties are unwilling or unable, I would like my pets to be cared for at the local animal shelter, ______________________________,

for the remainder of their lives.

Additional Animals

In the event I have additional animals such as chickens, goats, cows, horses, or other farm animals that aren't part of a farm business, I would like them to be treated as part of my estate. Unless my will, trust, or a letter of instruction directs differently, please ask if family, friends, or neighbors would agree to take them. If not, they may be sold or given to a breed-specific shelter.

These animals' identification tags and numbers are: ______________________________

____

____

____

____

Miscellaneous Information and Instructions

I have a storage unit(s) located at: ______________________________

____

It is owned by: ______________ Phone number: ______________

The keys are located: ______________________________

Heirlooms, Art, Jewelry, and Other Objects

Heirlooms, art, jewelry, and other objects should be inventoried (items should be photographed and insured, if appropriate). Consider mentioning these in your estate plan, if one exists.

1. Descriptions of my heirlooms, art, jewelry, and other objects of value.

____

____

____

____

____

Miscellaneous Information and Instructions, cont.

Heirlooms, Art, Jewelry, and Other Objects, cont.

Personal property should be distributed as provided in my will or letter of instruction in my estate planning documents as part of the estate adminisration.

2. I have hidden valuables, which are listed below along with their location:

____

____

____

____

3. My clothing should be disposed of as follows:

____

____

4. Perishable and nonperishable food should be given to:

____

____

Consider identifying the location of and people in your photographs for future generations. Share copies (either physical or electronic) with your family members to help preserve family history.

Personal and Confidential Information

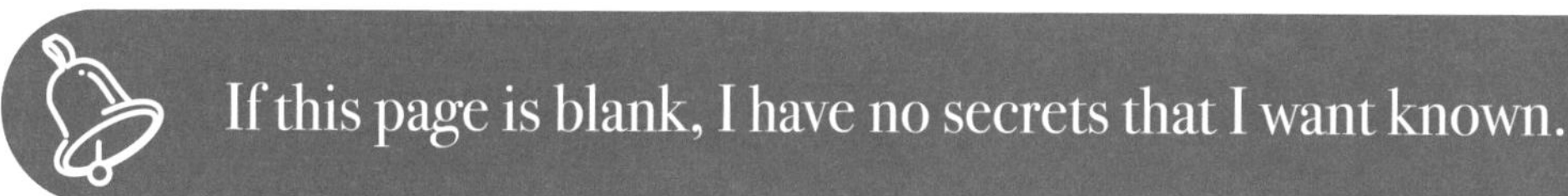
If this page is blank, I have no secrets that I want known.

There may be information about or confessions relating to me that I deemed private or delicate in nature, but may pertain to my estate. It is not my intent to cause harm or discomfort to anyone, only to fully disclose information pertaining to my estate.

I have written that information down, including all available details, and secured it at or with (suggestions: attorney or safety-deposit box):

This information should be delivered to ____,

whose contact information is ____

____.

This information may contain secret bank accounts, information regarding relationships, apartments, collections, and other property—both personal and real. My instructions contain a description or information regarding the items and the appropriate disposition or handling of such information. It is my specific intent that the recipient of this information be as discreet as possible with such personal items and/or information so as not to cause undue harm or unnecessary embarrassment to others or myself.

Caution: Do not use this information to pass any property of value, as the property may not pass as intended and may need to be disclosed to the executor, personal representative, trustee, and/or court for legal reporting purposes.

Section II

What to Do with My Estate When I'm No Longer Here

Initial Administration Steps

There are certain things that need to be done after arrangements for the funeral or memorial are finalized, such as locating the estate planning documents. In the planning documents, you should find the name of the chosen personal representative, successor trustee, or fiduciary who is to assist with the administration. However, if there are no planning documents, most states require a court appointment before a person has the authority to act on behalf of a decedent.

Regardless of whether or not a representative has been selected, there are certain things that need to be done to secure the estate. One of the most important tasks is making certain that all personal property is protected. Unfortunately, there have been cases where family members or friends have removed items of value that should have been inventoried as part of the estate. An example is a case of a brother who rented a truck and packed it full of every valuable he could find, while his sister, the appointed fiduciary, was making funeral arrangements. As audacious as this sounds, it does happen.

Immediate Care of Property

There are two types of property:

1. Real property, which is land and whatever is attached to it, like a house
2. Personal property, which is any property—tangible or intangible—other than real property

1. SECURE ALL PROPERTY

It is extremely important that nothing is disturbed or removed from the decedent's property (at home or elsewhere) unless it is necessary for safekeeping. Items, small and large, commonly disappear following a death. If protection of assets is a concern, it is wise to contact an attorney to ask for guidance.

Most homeowners have several sets of keys to their property, which might be in the possession of several different people including family members, friends, neighbors, nurses, housekeepers, and custodians. If the decedent lived alone, a prudent first step may be to change the locks and implement additional security measures such as automatically timed lights. If the decedent had a home security system, it would be wise to change the codes.

Cancel newspapers or other scheduled deliveries and arrange for someone to collect the mail daily, as stacks of newspapers and a stuffed mailbox are indicators that no one is home.

2. INVENTORY PROPERTY

If death occurred in the hospital or care facility, request a list of personal property belonging to the decedent. Use the list to identify what may still be at the facility. If the property was returned to someone, determine who took possession.

Make an inventory list of personal property. Include things like jewelry, television(s), computer(s), painting(s), sculpture(s), etc. At some point the personal representative or executor will need the listed items. These records are crucial for proper administration of the estate.

3. LOCATE ESTATE PLANNING DOCUMENTS

This book should help you locate the documents (see page 40). If there is a family attorney, he or she will probably have the documents or at least know where they are located. Family or friends can also assist in finding the decedent's written instructions. This book should indicate where these documents should be found.

In some cases, more than one estate plan may surface. If this happens, each will need to be examined by an attorney or, perhaps, even a court to determine which plan governs. Usually the last validly signed documents will control the estate proceedings.

If a valid estate plan cannot be located, the person is said to have died intestate. In that case, state law should be consulted to determine who receives the property.

When death was anticipated, locating the estate planning documents may be easy, if they exist. If death was unexpected, a more comprehensive search may be required. Safeguarding these documents is as important as securing and safeguarding property. Unauthorized alteration or destruction of estate planning documents is against the law.

Identify the Personal Representative, Executor, or Trustee

A fiduciary may be referred to as a personal representative, executor, or trustee. This is the person who will manage and close the affairs of the decedent and the estate. The estate planning documents should identify who has been chosen to be the fiduciary. They should be notified of the death.

If there are no estate planning documents, most states have laws that list, in order, who may apply to become a fiduciary when none is appointed. Some jurisdictions allow anyone, even creditors, to petition to be such representatives. The court has the ultimate authority in such appointment processes and it might be best to contact an attorney to help you identify the proper fiduciary.

Should you require legal advice, don't be afraid to interview attorneys. Ask about fees and estimated hours involved.

Estate planning documents will dictate what type of administration is required. With a will, a small estate affidavit, small estate probate, or regular probate may need to be initiated. If a living trust was created and funded with property, the appointed trustee will administer the trust. Sometimes assets will simply pass automatically if they have an identified beneficiary, are held jointly, or pass by a transfer on death (TOD) or payable on death (POD) designation.

A more in-depth definition of probate can be found on page 107.

UNDERSTANDING FIDUCIARY OBLIGATIONS AND DUTIES:

Once the proper fiduciary is identified, that person will take over all administrative duties for the estate or trust, as the case may be. They will have certain duties and responsibilities, one of which is to keep the heirs and beneficiaries updated with status reports. In some cases, the fiduciary may be required to obtain a bond to guarantee that the individual will act appropriately.

Fiduciary responsibilities are reviewed in more detail on page 84.

Disposition of Remains

Follow the decedent's wishes for disposition of the body (cremation or burial). See pages 23–33 for additional details about the mortuary and memorial services. If the decedent left no instructions, consult state law. In most jurisdictions, when valid instructions do not exist, the family makes the decision relating to disposition, although this issue sometimes is ripe for dispute.

If the family cannot agree, legal conflict can arise, causing anguish and undue expense. Let the appointed fiduciary guide those involved. If there is any question about disposition of the body, contact an attorney for assistance. When disputes arise over disposition of the body, realize that this is one task that cannot be altered, so there should be no mistakes.

Consult an Attorney

The fiduciary should contact an attorney to discuss administration and closing of the estate, as there are many pitfalls and traps for the inexperienced. Protect yourself by asking for help if you are charged with the responsibility of a fiduciary role because if this is not done right, the fiduciary might face personal liability for claims by creditors, heirs, or beneficiaries.

Call Social Security

The Social Security office should be notified as soon as possible. A death benefit payment may be available. If the decedent was receiving benefits, you may need to reimburse the government for benefits that were received after death.

To report the death to Social Security call 1-800-722-1213.

Take Time to Reflect and Relax

During an emotional process, everyone needs time. Get plenty of rest. There is greater likelihood of tempers flaring and disputes arising if you are sleep-deprived and stressed. Taking time to relax and reflect may also help you work through your grief because it is during quiet times that people begin to reinforce positive memories of those no longer with us. It is easy to get trapped in a "work more" or "control" mindset as an escape, but these behaviors are actually disguised grieving experiences.

It's important to understand that you may feel overwhelmed; these feelings are natural. Be slow and deliberate about the tasks ahead in order to care for yourself and those you love. Sometimes a short trip or even an afternoon drive to a calm and peaceful location can refresh you enough to move forward.

Fiduciary Responsibilities

Fiduciaries are people in a position of trust and duty, but there are several types. They might be referred to as the personal representative, executor, trustee, or any combination of the three but, no matter the label, they have the legal responsibilities of a fiduciary. A personal representative generally handles the administration of the estate through probate; an executor typically works with an intestate person's estate, which may also require probate; and a trustee handles trust administration matters. They are all fiduciaries, and their standards are spelled out in state law. Different titles may exist in different states.

The duties of a fiduciary are important and, as such, the person selected should be chosen for their good judgment and history of reasonable actions. A fiduciary must be responsible, honest, prudent, impartial, and patient, as they will probably be called upon to identify, collect, preserve, and protect property and handle the business of the estate.

Some of the Responsibilities a Fiduciary Might Face

The duties of a fiduciary will not be accomplished quickly. They may take months. It's always best to calmly move forward with knowledge and a plan.

1. Notify devisees, heirs, and creditors of probate proceedings if the estate is in probate (see page 107). Also, notify banks, stockbrokers, insurance agencies, the family accountant and family lawyer, and any other pertinent persons of the death (see pages 21 and 34–39).

2. Take possession of, inventory, and preserve the decedent's assets. Collect benefits of life insurance, veteran's benefits, and refunds on prepaid services such as magazine subscriptions. Prepare an inventory and obtain a valuation or appraisal of assets. Make sure the assets are properly insured. The estate should continue to pay homeowner's insurance on

property and auto insurance on vehicles until these assets are sold or otherwise disposed of. You may need to get a rider on any homeowner's insurance if the property will be vacant. Contact your insurance agent in this regard.

3. The fiduciary may need to establish an estate account for the collection of income and payment of bills. This may not be necessary in certain circumstances, such as when a surviving spouse had a joint account with the decedent and the surviving spouse is entitled to all the assets. However, if the surviving spouse requires assistance in managing the assets, they may choose to seek the assistance of an accountant or bookkeeper or someone they trust. That is a personal decision that should be made by the spouse.

   The fiduciary may also need to obtain a tax identification number for the estate, which will substitute for a Social Security number. It is not appropriate to use the decedent's Social Security number after death. During their lifetimes, people use Social Security numbers to track income activity and tax reporting. After death, a tax identification number, to be used solely for the estate and/or trust, replaces it. Use IRS form SS-4, which can be found on the IRS website: www.irs.gov.

4. Collect all income, such as rents, interest, or dividends, as well as all debts, claims, salary, and notes due the decedent. Deposit this income into the estate account. Do not mix the estate assets and income with your personal funds during administration. A fiduciary should keep a separate book detailing the accounting of the estate assets.

5. Determine the names, ages, locations, and degrees of relationship of all heirs, devisees, and beneficiaries. Care and caution must be exercised here. If there is a will or trust, the devisees, heirs, and beneficiaries should be easy to identify, although many court cases exist based on improper distribution to the wrong heirs or beneficiaries. If no planning documents exist, state law will determine who receives estate property.

6. Complete any legal actions in which the decedent had an interest. Represent the estate in any challenges to the will.

7. Calculate and file tax returns, and pay all state and federal income, inheritance, and estate taxes in a timely manner. There are many different forms and deadlines to watch out for here, so seek help from a tax attorney or accountant. Do not risk penalties and interest by failing to get these done on time. There may be separate income tax returns required for the estate (as a separate entity) and any trust. A good rule of thumb is to check during the first thirty days after death. For example, where appropriate, consider exercising a disclaimer, which must be made within nine months after death.

8. Pay valid creditor claims. Investigate all claims to determine whether they are legitimate debts. Deny invalid claims. Payment of invalid claims may cause liability to the fiduciary for improper distribution. If questions arise about claims, the fiduciary has the responsibility to investigate. Publication of the death (other than an obituary) in a paper of general circulation may be required to put unknown creditors on notice and give them an opportunity to bring a claim against the estate. Failure to publish a notice could lead to liability for claims months or years after the estate is closed. If assets were distributed, the fiduciary could be found personally liable for improper distributions. This notice (which usually has a special form) should be published as soon as legally and practically possible.

9. When necessary, sell property at fair market value to raise funds to settle claims, taxes, and administration expenses.

10. Transfer property as specifically designated by the decedent to certain people at the appropriate time. In some cases, you need court authority before making a distribution. In all cases, it is important to get a distribution receipt to prove the distribution was made. It is a good idea to consult an attorney before making distributions to determine how the timing of the distribution might affect the estate in terms of taxes and creditor claims.

11. When appropriate, distribute the rest of the estate to those entitled to the estate or trust property either under the planning documents or as defined by intestacy law. Consult state statutes on the property distribution order if the planning documents do not provide for an order of distribution.

12. File a declaration of completion of probate with the appropriate court if probate is required. In a trust administration, most states do not require such a declaration. However, the fiduciary should send a letter to the beneficiaries informing them that the administration process has concluded.

13. Notify all heirs or beneficiaries that the estate is closed. Seek a discharge of fiduciary responsibility from the court.

14. Throughout the process, keep accurate records and books for reporting to the court and beneficiaries when appropriate.

15. Communicate, communicate, communicate.

If you are confused over any part of the process, seek the advice of an attorney. If you or the estate does not have an attorney, interview several. Prepare a list of questions and items you might need assistance with, such as court filings, then make several calls. In most cases an attorney or their aide will outline how they can be of assistance and what their fees entail. You are hiring this person on behalf of the estate and it is important to find a knowledgeable person you can communicate with.

You should also familiarize yourself with state laws, as these affect what type of estate you have and how the process unfolds. There is a reference page at the back of the book to help you locate governing state laws.

Why Would I Want to Be a Fiduciary?

Being a fiduciary is a responsibility that should not be taken lightly. Many have asked what the advantages are of being in that position. It is true that in some cases a fiduciary is paid for their service; however, a fiduciary is usually a family member or friend. They usually agree to accept the position because they cared about the individual and feel a sense of honor in being asked to hold the appointment. In a way, it is a tribute to the deceased to make certain that what they had achieved in life is properly cared for after death.

Estate Property

Identifying and Caring for the Estate Property and Its Obligations

One of the responsibilities of a fiduciary includes identifying and caring for the estate property. In the following section is a list of property that is involved in many estates. The list is not all-inclusive, and identification of property will vary depending on each estate. In addition to identifying special forms of property, the following also discloses proper handling and disposition of the property.

Real Property

Real property is land and homes or buildings that are on the land. Real property is titled in an owner's name at the county recorder's office in the county where the land is located. There is a process to transfer land to devisees, heirs, and/or beneficiaries:

1. Determine how the decedent owned the land. Is it held outright by the decedent, as joint tenants with a right of survivorship, or in some other form such as a trust? If the property was owned jointly with right of survivorship, the joint owner should first check with state law then report the death to the county recorder's office and work to remove the decedent's name from title. Most counties require you to file a new deed, which requires a death certificate. There will be a fee but if a decedent's name is not taken off the deed to real property, it can cause a real hassle for the heirs who try to clear up the title later on.

2. If the property is owned solely by the decedent, the fiduciary of the estate must transfer the property to the rightful heirs, devisees, and/or beneficiaries at the conclusion of the administrative process. The fiduciary uses written authorization from the court, called the letters of testamentary or letters of administration, to prepare and sign new deeds to the property and file them at the county recorder's office. Sometimes an abbreviated process may be available.

Check with local counsel. Distribution of property should not occur until the law or court authorizes distribution. An attorney can help you determine the right timing.

3. In some cases, the estate may not have enough liquid funds to cover all the liabilities. When this happens, the fiduciary may need to mortgage or sell the real property of the estate or trust. Remember, a fiduciary has a legal responsibility to act in the best interest of the estate or trust. The fiduciary should not sell the property at prices well below market value to friends, relatives, or themself.

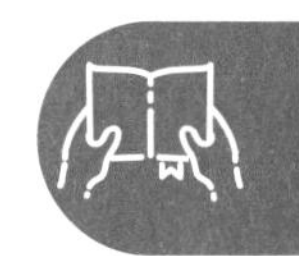

4. If the property has mortgages or other liens, the fiduciary will need to contact the lender or lien holder and work out payment. Many lenders will require that regular payments continue during the administration of the estate, but check with the lender. If payments have to continue, the fiduciary will have to arrange for these payments with other estate assets unless an immediate distribution to the beneficiary is appropriate.

   Generally, mortgages are not transferable, so if a beneficiary wants a home that has a mortgage, the beneficiary may need to refinance the mortgage in the beneficiary's name.

5. If property is held in a trust, consult the trust document for proper disposition of the property. New deeds may need to be issued. Mortgage issues are generally addressed in the same manner as outlined in number 4 above.

The transfer of real property is a legal act and must be done carefully at the proper time. The assistance of qualified counsel is highly recommended. This professional will know how to avoid problems if title to the property is not clear or will know what to do about title insurance. Also, the form of the deed to sign is very important. Many states and counties have different types of deeds for different purposes. If a wrong deed is used, there could be negative consequences such as unintended liability for warranties made as a result of the form.

Pets

On pages 69–70 the decedent may have listed their wishes for the care of their pets. That list might include cats, dogs, fish, hamsters, or even snakes, and in some cases farm animals.

1. Determine if there are any animals that are not pets. A herd of cattle will not receive the same treatment as a family dog. Livestock is an asset of the estate, to be disposed of like other personal property. A pet does not generally have great monetary value unless it's a champion breed animal.

2. Identify whether the decedent left any instruction about how they wanted the pet(s) cared for. Some state laws allow for "pet trusts" or other special instructions. In these cases, the specific directions shall be followed. Keep in mind that some states do not allow people to leave money to their pets. Check state law.

3. Contact the beneficiaries of the estate and tell them the plan for the pet, if there is one. If there is no plan, ask for volunteers to care for the pet. If no one volunteers, reach out to friends and other family members before placing a call to the local humane society or animal shelter for assistance.

4. If there are disputes among the beneficiaries or heirs about who gets Fido, he should be cared for with estate expenses until they can work out an agreement or the court decides.

5. Deliver the pet(s) to the new owner. All reasonable belongings should go with the pet (i.e., doghouse, bowls, food, etc.). Do not distribute nontraditional pet items along with the pet. Just because Kitty Cat liked to watch television doesn't mean the television should be distributed with the cat.

6. Write down who received the pet(s) and the accessories in the administrative records you should be keeping. Eventually, the fiduciary should deliver this accounting of property to their attorney and/or accountant.

Bank Accounts

1. Determine how bank accounts were held by the decedent. If they owned them solely, the asset is distributed according to the estate plan or the law. The fiduciary will need to provide official court documents and/or a death certificate to the bank to prove they have the authority to access and distribute those funds.

   If there is a joint account with right of survivorship, the co-owner should be notified of the death. All the money in the account automatically passes to the survivor and is now owned by the survivor. The account is not considered part of the probate estate property except for tax purposes and the co-owner should be aware that there might be tax consequences when they get full ownership. The fiduciary should remember to track account income and principal separately, which is necessary for tax calculations.

   If the account is held in trust, the successor trustee should have access to the account. They will need to show the bank the trust or court documents showing authority to act on behalf of the trust.

2. The fiduciary may need to transfer funds from the decedent's bank accounts into an estate bank account in order to deposit estate income and to pay estate bills or other expenses. The fiduciary will need to get a federal tax identification number (IRS Form SS-4) to open the estate account.

3. Do not distribute money from an estate without authority or as allowed by statute. Court approval may be required before making a distribution. Any interim distributions should be recorded in the fiduciary's records for estate property. After all estate expenses and obligations have been paid, the estate account should be the last item distributed to heirs and beneficiaries.

Stocks and Bonds

1. Notify the broker or financial planner of the death. Obtain date-of-death valuations. It is very important to obtain the actual date-of-death value of any accounts. In fact, for tax purposes, the high, low, and close on the day of death needs to be obtained for individu-

ally held securities. The broker should be able to provide such a report. If stock certificates are found and no broker is associated with the certificates, the fiduciary will either need to contact an appropriate transfer agent or hire a broker to handle the transfer of the certificates. Contacting the company that issued the certificates originally may also lead to finding a transfer agent. If the company no longer exists, contact a broker to determine if any value still exists.

2. As with bank accounts, determine the proper ownership of the stocks and bonds. If there are co-owners who hold the investments jointly with rights of survivorship, then the co-owners automatically receive the assets, and the property is not part of the probate estate, but it is still inventoried for tax purposes.

3. Speak to the attorney, broker, or financial planner about the plan for distribution of the assets. It is important that distribution be done as the decedent intended. For example, if the decedent wanted his blue-chip stocks to be distributed intact to the beneficiaries for long-term holding, that should be done.

4. If needed, the fiduciary may request a liquidation of some stocks and/or bonds to pay estate expenses. Contact the broker or financial advisor in charge of the accounts if this action is appropriate.

5. Remember that the fiduciary has a duty to protect and preserve estate assets. Discuss the portfolio with the broker or financial planner and adjust accordingly. Be conservative but not overly protective. Reasonableness of investment is the key to proper administration.

6. At the appropriate time, and after court approval when required, the fiduciary should either cash out the stocks and bonds and distribute the proceeds to the heirs or transfer the investments directly to the heirs. This decision should be made jointly between the fiduciary and the specified beneficiaries.

Automobiles and Other Vehicles of Title

1. Make sure that the vehicles are properly stored or protected. Do not drive the vehicle or allow it to be driven unnecessarily. Any driver of the vehicle is responsible to the estate or trust (and the ultimate beneficiaries) for any damage done. Be sure insurance continues.

2. When disposition is appropriate or after a court order if necessary, contact the DMV, fill out a change of title form, and attach letters of testamentary and/or administration. The fiduciary has the authority to sign on behalf of the decedent. Some states offer expedited procedures for changing title. Check your local laws for expedited procedures for changing titles.

3. As with other assets, if the vehicle is held jointly with a right of survivorship, the survivor is entitled to the vehicle. The title change instructions in step 2 may not apply except to have the decedent's name removed from the title. Making sure the title is accurate is important for any future sale of the vehicle.

4. If there is a loan on the vehicle, contact the lender to determine the proper process for paying off the debt and ask that payments be suspended during the administration of the estate. If the lender will not agree to defer payment, the fiduciary will need to make arrangements to either continue payments from estate funds or to sell the vehicle. As with real property, the estate should receive fair market value for the vehicle. For example, a fiduciary should not sell a decedent's new Porsche to himself/herself for $500; that's a breach of fiduciary duties. The beneficiaries do have recourse through the courts if the fiduciary does not uphold their responsibilities.

Income and Payments to the Estate

1. Contact the decedent's employer (if applicable) to check for automatic deposit of paychecks, bonuses, and benefits. If the decedent was employed at the time of death, the estate should be paid for all work done up until the time of death. The HR department should be able to provide valuable information about any benefits that exist.

2. Contact the local Social Security office to cancel benefits if they were being paid to the decedent. Find out if a Social Security death benefit is available when calling to cancel any lifetime, age, or disability benefits.

   If the deceased was receiving Social Security benefits, you must return the benefit received for the month of death and any later months. For example, if the person died in July, you must return the benefits paid in July and August. The Social Security office will be able to assist you with information as to the best way to return overpayments.

   Do not cash any social security checks received for the month in which the person dies or later.

3. Check for insurance policies, which may or may not be considered income to the estate for income tax purposes. Look for these specific insurance policies:

   - Disability insurance
   - Credit card insurance (to automatically pay off balances at death)
   - Workers' compensation insurance
   - Death benefits provided by an employer
   - Unemployment benefits
   - Mortgage insurance that pays off the mortgage in the event of death
   - Life insurance

Death benefits from life insurance generally pass to beneficiaries income tax–free and are not considered income to the estate. However, the amount of the death benefit must be included as an asset of the estate if the decedent had the power to change the beneficiary.

Income or payments to the estate should usually be deposited to the estate account, with few exceptions. One of these exceptions might be money that was earned while the decedent was alive that was usually deposited into a joint account with the spouse. In this case, the income should be deposited in that joint account. Any income earned after death belongs to the estate and should be deposited into the estate account.

Some life insurance policies or deferred compensation plans will pay benefits directly to the named beneficiaries. It is very important for estate tax purposes that the fiduciary keep track of these benefits and include their record in the estate accounting. Failure to include these can result in tax liability and penalties.

The fiduciary might want to consult with an attorney if it is unclear where income should be deposited. It is important to correctly track income for tax purposes. If income is paid to a person, an IRS form 1040 and state income tax forms may be required. Income paid to the estate or trust may necessitate an IRS form 1041 and state tax forms.

Obligations of the Estate

Much of the following information can be located in the first section of this book.

1. Identify the decedent's creditors:

    - Doctors, hospitals, and care facilities
    - Funeral home or provider
    - Accountants and attorneys
    - Secured creditors such as mortgage holders
    - Unsecured creditors such as normal bills (see below)

2. Sort through the decedent's mail to identify bills from other creditors, which should be forwarded to the fiduciary:

Mortgage	Electric company
Loans	Sewer
Credit cards	Garbage
Internet provider	Water
Phone and cellular bills	Gas
Insurance	Yard/tree service
Taxes	Memberships and subscriptions

Obviously, not everyone is going to have all of the above bills, and some decedents may have other obligations not listed.

For each of these creditors, contact the account manager and notify that person of the death. The fiduciary should continue paying for services that are necessary for preservation of the estate assets and cancel all others. For example, unless the continuation is necessary to preserve assets, an internet account should be canceled.

For accounts that are kept open, request that the account reflect a name change to "Estate of (decedent)." You may be required to send the letters of administration with the request to prove that the person is deceased and that the estate is a valid entity.

It is important to recognize that not all creditors' claims may be valid. The fiduciary may want to speak to an attorney about how to determine whether a claim is valid and how to deny it if you do not believe it should be paid.

3. Contact the decedent's bank to cancel automatic withdrawals, and also notify the creditor of the action taken. This is to prevent the bank account from being overdrawn.

The fiduciary must make a diligent search for all claimants, who must be notified of their right to assert claims against the estate. Some states require the fiduciary to file an affidavit of compliance sixty days after this search and notification is complete. State law will define the time limit in which creditors must file their claims after they are notified of their right to do so.

Miscellaneous

1. Organ donations must be acted on in a timely manner. The wishes of the decedent and a sample form can be located on pages 6–7 or in other estate documents.

2. If not already done, obtain a list of personal effects kept by the care facility or hospital. Most hospitals will inventory glasses, rings, etc. upon admission. Locate identified items. Also begin making a list of personal effects around the home (see number 7 on the next page.)

3. Check for safety-deposit boxes and inventory their contents. The location of these should be listed on page 62. If not, look for receipts for payment of the boxes or ask the decedent's banker.

4. Check for safes or other hidden items of property around the house of the deceased. The average American keeps around $600 on hand somewhere in the house. Many times, cash may be stored in a coffee can in the freezer or hidden in book collections. Vents and behind photos or paintings are also common places to store "emergency" cash.

5. Check for rented storage lockers or other off-site storage locations. You may discover these through billing statements or receipts or you may need to ask family members if such storage exists.

6. If an inventory turns up illegal drugs or firearms requiring a permit, the fiduciary must take steps to protect the estate and himself/herself. Immediately notify the authorities, surrender the item(s) as required, and get a receipt.

7. Give the heirs and beneficiaries a list of personal property (such as furniture, clothing, and other personal effects) not mentioned in the estate plan. At the appropriate time, allow them to divide the property by agreement or as the decedent requested if instructions were given. If the estate has particularly valuable items or if there is a dispute as to who should receive certain things, the fiduciary may need to get court approval for distribution. Sometimes, valuable property needs to be sold to the highest bidder among the beneficiaries or others (with funds going to the estate).

   If the estate planning documents call for specific distributions of property, notify the heirs you will comply with the plan. Keep track of the fair market value of the items, as it may be important for tax filings. Also, if the estate owes more than it owns, you may need to hold an estate sale in order to pay creditors. In this circumstance, no distributions should be made.

Generally speaking, the IRS and the courts do not concern themselves with personal property unless it has value or there is a dispute about distribution. If either situation applies, you should estimate the value of the property (or obtain a professional estimate) and report the value to the IRS, state authority, and courts.

Before distributing personal property, consult an attorney to make sure you do it right. For tax reasons, make sure that all property distributions have been recorded. Once the value of property is determined and it is clear that there are enough other assets in the estate to satisfy claims, go ahead and distribute the personal effects.

If there is leftover property that no one wants, it might be appropriate to have an estate sale. Remember that all proceeds of the sale belong to the estate and go into the estate account.

There are always miscellaneous items that remain after distribution or sale of property and some that just don't fit into any other category. If they have not been noted in the first section of *About Me*, you might consider donating those to charitable organizations. An example is food. Foods that remain at the decedent's residence should be shared by the family or given to a charity such as a homeless shelter. Food is one of the few things that can be given before the estate administration is closed. Items like dishes, flatware, and other kitchen utensils can usually be donated to domestic abuse shelters. Arts and crafts supplies are also generally welcome at shelters. Blankets are always received at homeless shelters and old towels can find new purpose in animal shelters.

The simple act of giving during this difficult time actually contributes to your own overall healing process.

What If There Was a Business?

Hopefully, if the decedent had a business, there will be some estate planning to state what should be done with the business at the time of death. This is another area in which an attorney's assistance will be very important.

Generally, the fiduciary has great latitude in handling the decedent's business affairs and for all practical purposes takes the place of the decedent. The only caveat is that the fiduciary must continue to operate and act reasonably for the best interests of the beneficiaries. It is vital to preserve the value of the business or venture.

The fiduciary must determine whether the corporation or business has adequate management to maintain its value and whether there is an agreement addressing death. This determination is much more important in a closely held corporation or business where the decedent was the majority owner. Publicly traded companies and most larger corporations or businesses will likely have internal procedures to deal with the death of a key person.

These are some things a fiduciary should consider when an estate includes ownership of a business:

1. **Gather the necessary information to make a good decision.**

   Was the decedent a key person? Will there be someone to manage the corporation? Is the corporation profitable and will it remain profitable past the decedent's death? Can the assets or stocks be sold at a fair price? Look for a buy-sell or shareholder agreement that addresses sale of the stock. Stocks may be either held or sold and sometimes must be sold.

2. **Decide what to do with the business.**

   The fiduciary must determine the best course for the beneficiaries. Should the business or corporation be continued, merged, sold, or liquidated? Shares are treated like any other investment.

3. Decide when to act.

Time is critical. The business may be losing value each day the decedent is not there to run it. Look to agreements for deadlines. Usually, the stock will be disposed of with other estate assets.

4. Control the assets.

Assets of the business may need to be protected and accounted for. The fiduciary may have responsibility beyond the disposal of the stock.

Partnerships may be handled differently than corporations. In a true "partnership" context, the estate may receive a decedent's partnership interest. That does not mean that the estate is automatically entitled to the decedent's share of partnership assets. First, locate the partnership agreement. This document should tell what is to be done upon the death of a partner. If a partnership agreement does not exist, state laws have provisions for managing a partnership without written agreement or where the agreement does not apply.

Laws dealing with partnership disposition vary widely from state to state. It is very important to consult with a professional to navigate through this process.

If the decedent was a professional, the fiduciary may face the challenge of what to do with numerous client or patient records. A good place to start is the state professional association. They can provide guidelines and recommendations on how to handle such records. Consultation with an attorney in this case is strongly recommended so the estate can avoid liability.

The fiduciary should also consider a business's or professional's accounts receivable. It is in the best interest of the beneficiaries to collect accounts receivable as soon as possible, as the value of the receivables may decrease over time.

What If the Estate Is Insolvent?

In some estates, debts from claims, taxes, and expenses exceed the value of the estate property. Generally speaking, when an estate is insolvent, there is nothing to be distributed to the heirs or beneficiaries because any property in the estate must be used to pay creditors, taxes, and expenses. The fiduciary is required to sell any estate property to satisfy these obligations. Most states have laws that specify the procedures for handling an insolvent estate. Examine these statutes carefully before even suggesting distributions to creditors.

State law may allow payment of support to the surviving spouse and dependent children from an insolvent estate. These payments must be approved by the court and usually may not continue after a certain period of time. Therefore, it is important that the spouse and dependent children take measures during that period to provide for themselves after the support payments from the estate cease.

If the estate is insolvent (there are no assets to pay debts), the fiduciary should send a letter to creditors informing them that the debtor has died and no estate assets exist to pay the debt. If the estate is in probate, it is important for the fiduciary to follow these steps:

1. Identify all creditors and estate assets.
2. Formulate a distribution plan of remaining assets and work with the creditors.
3. Seek court approval for the distribution plan.
4. Distribute assets in accordance with the court-approved plan.
5. Inform remaining creditors that decedent has no other assets and the accounts should be closed.

If no probate is involved, court approval for distribution may or may not be necessary, depending on the size of the debts in comparison to the size of the estate. In many cases, the fiduciary may notify the creditors of the estate's financial situation and request that the creditors discharge the debt.

To avoid liabilities, the fiduciary may want to consult an attorney when creditors pursue collection from an insolvent estate or about payment of estate assets to creditors.

All this may seem overwhelming. Don't rush through the process, seek advice from professionals, and take time for yourself. Those simple steps will make it all much easier.

Section III

Probate and Taxes

What Is Probate and Why Is It Necessary?

Probate is the legal process to transfer property from an owner no longer living to those who survive. The court supervises the process with the following goals:

1. Determine ownership of property
2. Appoint a person to legally transfer property
3. Provide an orderly transfer of property
4. Avoid temptation for fraud

Probate may be necessary for any of these actions:

1. Collecting, or taking possession of, the decedent's property
2. Protecting and preserving the decedent's estate
3. Paying all debts, claims, and taxes
4. Determining who is entitled to the assets and distributing them accordingly

Probate proceedings are not required for all estates. Circumstances that determine whether probate is needed include the size of the estate, the nature of the assets, the type of estate planning done, and the relationship of the decedent to the survivors.

For example, small estates (defined by statute) may not need to be formally probated. In this case, one or more of the decedent's "claiming successors" (i.e., heir or devisee) can file an affidavit of small estate with the court. With court authorization, the beneficiaries can then transfer property without going through a long and formal probate. The fiduciary should check with the state or with an attorney to determine if the estate is small enough for this faster probate option. If the estate qualifies, the probate attorney should recommend this abbreviated process, as it is usually much faster and less expensive than a normal probate.

When probate is necessary, all proceedings are subject to the jurisdiction and supervision of the court unless the statutes provide for a different process. The proper location for the probate is usually the decedent's county of residence and where the property is located. In some cases, such as where the decedent owned property in multiple states, the fiduciary may need to open multiple probates to handle administration.

The court will not interfere with the day-to-day tasks of administering an estate. Day-to-day tasks may include paying bills, settling uncontested claims, selling estate assets where appropriate, filing tax returns, and paying taxes. The court acts as general overseer to make sure matters are handled fairly. It will ensure the fiduciary acts in the best interest of the beneficiaries and will provide instructions and dispute resolution along the way.

The duration of probate varies from case to case. In simple single-heir and no-creditor cases, probate will be a relatively short process. When heirs and/or creditors dispute the rights to the decedent's property, probate can take several years.

The first step in probate is to petition the proper court for admission of the will to probate (or declaration of an intestate estate if no will exists) and appointment of the proper fiduciary. This step should be taken immediately following death. The personal representative then notifies all interested parties such as creditors, heirs, beneficiaries, and others that he or she will be acting as the fiduciary. The court may require the fiduciary to obtain a bond before it will issue letters of administration or letters testamentary.

The bond may be required by state law to act as an insurance policy, guaranteeing that the fiduciary will carry out their duties in a proper fashion. If the fiduciary breaches this responsibility, those harmed may seek damages from the fiduciary's bond. The bond company will then pursue the fiduciary for reimbursements of any amounts it must pay.

Some states allow a fiduciary to avoid filing a bond if the decedent waived the requirement in the estate planning documents. This waiver statement can save the estate thousands of dollars in bond costs.

The court then seeks to determine that the fiduciary is the proper party to administer the estate. Once it has decided that the person who petitioned the court is qualified and has complied with statute, it then issues letters of administration or letters testamentary. These are the documents that authorize the fiduciary to act on behalf of the estate.

Following notices to interested parties of the fiduciary's appointment, the fiduciary must take some immediate steps, such as reporting to the court about a search for creditors. As discussed previously, the fiduciary may also need to publish notice of the death in a paper of general circulation and report to the court when publication occurred. This notice is a legal notice of the death, not an obituary.

Relatively soon following appointment, the fiduciary is required to submit an initial inventory of estate assets to the court. This step is often completed at the same time as appointment of a fiduciary because the bond amount is usually based on the amount of assets in the estate.

Once the initial steps of probate are completed, a waiting period for creditors to bring claims is usually required. The period varies from state to state but may be four months or longer.

The fiduciary may need to keep the court updated on the status of the probate through annual accountings and progress reports. These accountings and progress reports inform the court of estate assets and any potential distributions to creditors. The probate process continues until all property is accounted for and court-ordered distributions are made. The fiduciary will then officially close the estate by getting court approval of a special form filed to declare that the probate is complete and the fiduciary is discharged.

Probate is not an easy or quick process. There are reference pages at the end of the book that provide the websites for the laws and statutes of each state. This does not substitute for a knowledgeable attorney. Consultation with counsel who is experienced in probate matters is highly recommended.

What Taxes Are Involved?

A decedent's estate may be subject to death taxes. Whether these taxes are due depends on the value of the assets in the "taxable estate." Federal and state governments collect a lot of revenue from estate taxes, gift taxes, estate income taxes, generation-skipping transfer taxes, and other assessments and penalties.

Gift, estate, and inheritance taxes are assessments against the transfer of property to others. Gift taxes may be due for lifetime transfers. Estate taxes are taxes collected from the estate on the transfer of property at death. Inheritance taxes are the corresponding taxes due from those receiving property. There is no federal inheritance tax, but there is federal estate tax. Some states have neither estate nor inheritance tax. Some states have either an estate or an inheritance tax. Some states have both.

Estate and Inheritance Tax Returns

A determination will need to be made whether the estate owes estate and/or inheritance taxes. This is another area where states vary greatly in their laws. The appropriate state statutes should be checked. Keep in mind that having zero tax liability does not eliminate the requirement to file estate or inheritance tax returns.

Consultation with a professional tax advisor is strongly recommended. Tax laws change constantly. A professional advisor will be able to help you navigate the issues you may not be aware of. When an estate is planned properly and the tax forms completed accurately, taking advantage of all deductions and credits, literally hundreds of thousands of dollars in larger estates can be saved in taxes that would otherwise need to be paid without planning.

The Decedent's Income Tax Returns

Income taxes must be paid on any income earned before death. The decedent's last 1040 and corresponding state return must be completed and filed by April 15 of the year following death.

Even if there is no income tax due, complete and file a return. At the top of the first page of the forms, type the words "Last Tax Return, Date of Death (date)."

If joint income tax returns were previously filed, the return for the year of death may be done jointly. Type the words "Last Joint Tax Return, Date of Death of (decedent) was (date)" at the top of the first page.

Fiduciary Income Tax Returns

It is beyond the scope of this book to discuss how to complete fiduciary income tax returns. Contact a qualified tax professional to assist in identifying due dates and preparation of these returns.

If the fiduciary does not properly determine the tax liability and get the returns and payments in on time, the estate may be assessed substantial tax debt, interest, and penalties. The beneficiaries of the estate rely on the fiduciary to know and take care of these matters. It is therefore very important to keep accurate records and accountings for estates and trusts, as those records will be used to calculate tax returns. Fiduciary liability can arise in this area.

Legal Requirements

Do not be lulled into believing that the Internal Revenue Service or your state's department of revenue or taxation will simply ignore a decedent's family or have sympathy as a result of the death. The law requires tax returns to be filed. Failure to comply with the law and report accurately may have negative consequences to fiduciaries and beneficiaries. The IRS may not catch up with you until many years after the death, but there is a good chance any irregularities will eventually be noticed. When in doubt about whether returns are required, consult with a professional tax advisor.

Section IV

When Disputes Arise

When Disputes Arise

There are three common situations that lead to disputes during probate, trust, or estate administration. Either (a) the involved parties are having difficulty dealing with the emotions of losing a loved one, (b) the estate plan is ambiguous or there isn't one, or (c) someone is unfairly taking advantage of others.

One of the unfortunate consequences of disputes is that relationships can be damaged beyond repair. Sometimes it can be difficult to recognize that a death can be an opportunity to reach out to each other and strengthen relationships. Unfortunately, there will be those who, for whatever reason, seem to create havoc among friends and family.

Disputes over administrative issues take two forms: (a) the manner in which the estate is being handled or (b) distribution issues when particular properties or amounts distributed are not what was expected by heirs and beneficiaries.

How the disputes are handled depends greatly on the type of dispute, the size of the estate, and the parties involved. Listed below are the recommended methods for handling disputes.

Informal Discussions by Parties

Calling a family meeting and listening to the concerns of all parties can sometimes bridge differences. If people are allowed to explain their positions and suggest a course of action, an amicable resolution can be accomplished. Sometimes, people just need to know they are being heard and feel that they are taking part in the process.

When attempting this course of action, it is very important to understand each person's perspective. Take care to avoid hurt feelings in other family members or interested parties; don't make decisions without listening or let one person bully others into accepting a specific position. Remember, each person is dealing with their own grief and the loss of a loved one.

When informal discussion does not resolve issues, or it is clear that it would be a waste of time, then other resolution options are available.

Informal Mediation and Handling by Attorneys/Mediators

When utilizing informal mediation, each party may want to retain their own attorney. Typically, counsel will represent the administrator and a separate lawyer or lawyers will represent each beneficiary or heir. The attorneys can communicate the wishes of each participant in a professional context and attempt to reach an amicable resolution of the issues without being hindered by emotional reactions. An obvious drawback to this course of action is the cost involved.

Effective attorneys will advise on a reasonable course of action and keep their clients informed of the cost and status of ongoing discussions. This allows each client the opportunity to make good decisions on how to resolve the matter.

Formal Mediation with Mediator

If attorneys and their clients are unable to reach an amicable resolution of differences, they can hire a mediator or arbitrator, who are usually judges or lawyers with many years of experience in a particular area of practice. They are neutral third parties who listen to the facts of both sides and attempt to resolve the matter.

A successful mediation usually results in resolution of the issues so that both sides are either equally pleased or equally displeased with the result. Rarely does a party win mediation.

Because mediators focus on both the law and the facts, it is imperative to have counsel at the mediation to represent each person's interest. Failure to do so could result in an unacceptable result to the unrepresented party.

Court Petition Seeking Instructions

If a dispute simply involves a question of interpretation, some courts allow an interested party to petition the court for instructions or interpretation. Usually, all parties get notice of the petition and are given an opportunity to voice their position to the court.

The court petition option is a method to avoid a lengthy litigation and acts as a fast track for issue resolution. Not all courts offer this type of process or resolution, so state law and court procedure must be examined. And even if the law allows for this process, the judge may have the option to not make a decision.

Lawsuit

As a last resort, aggrieved parties may choose to file an action with the court. The lawsuit may seek injunctive relief, ask for monetary damages, or challenge the estate plan. This option is usually the most costly, both economically and emotionally. Additionally, the litigation process will probably take longer than any of the options listed above. When closure to an estate is important, litigation can prevent it from happening for months or even years.

If a dispute is anticipated, it is usually better to handle the issues immediately. A discussion about the problem may lead to a faster and more efficient resolution. If a dispute is still unavoidable, try to maintain personal relationships despite the stated differences, although at the lawsuit stage it may be too late.

Section V

Coping with the Loss of a Loved One

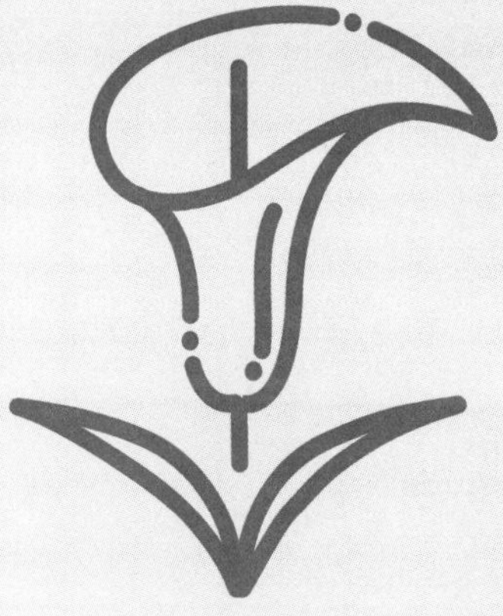

Coping with the Loss of a Loved One

Grief is something that is difficult to describe. There is no right way or wrong way to grieve because, although it's a natural reaction to loss, it's different for each person. It's not unusual to feel a wide range of emotions. Sometimes immediate sadness may be replaced by pleasant memories, even laughter. These emotions may seem contradictory, but it's all part of the healing process as human beings.

It's important to acknowledge that grief doesn't have a schedule, a set order of emotions, or any uniform response. It does, however, help us cope with loss. We each experience loss in our own unique way, and according to Mental Health America, a number of emotions may surface:

Denial	Disbelief
Confusion	Shock
Sadness	Yearning
Anger	Humiliation
Despair	Guilt

The emotions you experience are normal and part of the healing process. During the various stages of grief, one characteristic that is vitally important is courage. It takes courage to acknowledge the absence of a loved one and to continue on without that person.

Courage is required to express your feelings to others and to answer questions people may ask. Sometimes it takes courage just to get out of bed and face the day. It takes courage to work through the stages of grief. As the waves of grief come and go, like waves on a beach, some of the pain may subside, but for some, this process may take a long time. Don't force it. It is a natural process that expresses itself differently in each of us.

You may feel that things seem dreamlike or unreal, or you may feel isolated or distant from others, or you may feel that no one else really understands what you are going through. You may have frequent urges to cry. Try to relax with whatever you are feeling because it is all a normal response to loss. Such feelings demonstrate that you cared for and loved the person.

Acknowledging and encouraging these natural reactions will help you through the grief and mourning process.

It's best to try to be understanding of the normal stressors that everyone feels when a loved one passes. While you are grieving try to postpone any major decisions such as a move, job change, financial investment, or other major life changes. Avoid making hasty decisions—financial or otherwise—about the personal belongings of the deceased, which you may later regret. Circumvent emotional confrontations that may arise over belongings. If you feel pressured or pushed by anyone, tell them that you need a little time and space at the moment, that you aren't avoiding the issue but you'd like to discuss the issue later. Try to be gentle and remember that they are also feeling a sense of loss and everyone will react differently.

It's better for you if you avoid drugs or alcohol to numb what you're feeling. Avoidance of your feelings can prolong your sense of grief.

Positive and supportive things that can help the healing process include speaking openly with others, asking for help when you feel overwhelmed, and taking time to make important decisions. Celebrate the individual who passed and the fact that you had a relationship with such a valuable person by contributing to conversations with pleasant memories and heartfelt fondness. Focus on the good aspects of your relationship to the deceased and recall the times together that were joyful and emotionally constructive to you.

Be supportive of others and realize they are going through their own grief experience, but also keep boundaries for yourself. If there are times when you don't want to participate in a discussion, be honest, but firm, and simply say, "I don't want to get into that now." There may be some people who will push and not understand your request. That can usually be overcome by telling them that you need to process everything and would prefer to talk about it at another time. If you are firm, but gentle and direct, most people will accede to your request.

Above all, realize that you are not alone in what you are feeling. The scope of reactions and emotions doesn't have any boundaries. Death, and the grief that accompanies it in any form, is part of the natural process of life.

Children and Death

Questions from children about death can be some of the toughest you face. The difficulty arises because the questions seem so simple, but the answers can be difficult. Children are acutely aware of death and tragedy. At a minimum, they can pick up subtle emotional changes in parents and others around them and sense that something is wrong.

It is very important to try to communicate with a child in a manner they can understand. Use simple words and examples. Tell the truth. Be up front and do not let death become a "taboo" subject. Answer their questions as best you can, and do not be afraid to admit that you don't know something. You, too, can learn and experience with the child.

What you tell a child is a matter of personal judgment, morals, beliefs, and customs. The child looks to you to provide authority on the subject, so remember you are shaping a young person's beliefs and customs with the information and advice you give. It is important to be consistent and to set a good example.

Children also need reassurance that their caregivers will continue to be there for them during the time of grief and beyond. The most valuable things you can provide a child are your attention, your affection, and reassurance that they are loved.

While this book is not intended to be an authority on helping anyone cope with death, it is designed to help those who remain behind. Grieving is part of the process of healing. If you feel overwhelmed or need help, reach out. There are many helpful resources available, some of which have been listed at the back of this book. Don't be afraid to utilize them as healing tools that can be readily accessed.

Final Thoughts

The passing of someone you care about is one thing that cannot be avoided in life. It is traumatic, emotionally painful, and, beyond the loss, can cause a sense of disconnection. Grief can present itself in numerous ways and it can take on many different forms of expression. It is unique to each of us; there is no right or wrong way to experience it. While it's a very personal process, thinking straight may not be a realistic option at the time of a loved one's incapacitation or death, which is why this book has been invaluable to many.

About Me provides a compassionate path to follow when the one you love is not there to tell you what they want. It can act as a comforting guide to help navigate decisions while allowing the time and opportunity to grieve the loss that is felt. It's also a book that can be used by family and friends who, in the future, want to reconnect to that special someone who took the time to share their wishes on its pages.

I have watched as my clients moved through the processes of dealing with grief and the "must do" list pertaining to property and the estate. I've experienced it myself with the loss of my mother and others close to me. Those are the reasons I recommend two things to both the owner of and the recipient of *About Me*: (1) create an estate plan and (2) utilize this book as a companion to the estate plan to make a difficult time easier for those who remain.

Let *About Me* be a gift to pave the way through a tumultuous time.

Resources

Resources for Grief

Books about Grief

BOOKS FOR CHILDREN

Charlotte's Web by E. B. White, illustrated by Garth Williams (HarperCollins, 1952)

God Gave Us Heaven by Lisa Tawn Bergren, illustrated by Laura J. Bryant (WaterBrook, 2008)

The Goodbye Book by Todd Parr (Little, Brown and Company, 2015)

Ida, Always by Carol Levis and Charles Santoso (Atheneum Books for Young Readers, 2016)

I Miss You: A First Look at Death by Pat Thomas (Barron's, 2001)

The Invisible String by Patrice Karst, illustrated by Joanne Lew-Vriethoff (Little, Brown and Company, 2018)

I Will Always Love You by Melissa Lyons, illustrated by Mary Cindrich (Choose to Choose Inc., 2019)

The Sad Dragon: A Dragon Book about Grief and Loss by Steve Herman (DG Books Publishing, 2019)

Something Very Sad Happened: A Toddler's Guide to Understanding Death by Bonnie Zucker, illustrated by Kim Fleming (Magination Press, 2016)

Where Are You? A Child's Book about Loss by Laura Olivieri, illustrated by Kristin Elder (Lulu .com, 2007)

Why Do I Feel So Sad? A Grief Book for Children by Tracy Lambert, illustrated by Elena Napoli (Rockridge Press, 2020)

BOOKS FOR ALL AGES

Finding Meaning: The Sixth Stage of Grief by David Kessler (Scribner, 2019)

Graceful Passages: A Companion for Living and Dying by Michael Stillwater and Gary Malkin, producers (New World Library, 2006)

Grief Day By Day: Simple Practices and Daily Guidance for Living with Loss by Jan Warner (Althea Press, 2018)

It's OK That You're Not OK: Meeting Grief and Loss in a Culture That Doesn't Understand by Megan Devine (Sounds True, 2017)

On Death and Dying: What the Dying Have to Teach Doctors, Nurses, Clergy and Their Own Families by Elisabeth Kübler-Ross (Scribner, 2014)

On Grief and Grieving: Finding the Meaning of Grief through the Five Stages of Loss by Elisabeth Kübler-Ross and David Kessler (Scribner, 2005)

Please Be Patient, I'm Grieving: How to Care for and Support the Grieving Heart by Gary Roe (Self-published, GR Healing Resources, 2016)

Your Grief, Your Way: A Year of Practical Guidance and Comfort after Loss by Shelby Forsythia (Zeitgeist, 2020)

Community Resources

HOSPICE BEREAVEMENT SERVICES

If your loved one passed while under the care of hospice, contact them. They generally have extensively trained bereavement counselors who offer compassionate support. Some hospices have groups that explore feelings and emotions during the grief process.

SUPPORT GROUPS

Local support groups can help individuals and families better understand their personal experiences. Your local hospital may be able to recommend some.

LOCAL CLERGY

If you are a person of faith, deeply held religious beliefs might be a source of comfort and strength. Reach out to your priest, rabbi, minister, imam, or other religious leader. Many of these clergy receive specific training in grief counseling.

LICENSED PROFESSIONAL COUNSELORS

Sometimes, processing grief and working through any unresolved issues may take several years and require more intense help and treatment. No one can rush the grieving process, and a death can bring other issues to the surface. Licensed professional counselors can help you work through your grief as well as refine and develop coping skills to help you face additional challenges.

Online and General Resources

Association for Death Education and Counseling, 860-586-7503, adec.org

"Bereavement and Grief," Mental Health America, mhanational.org/bereavement-and-grief

"The Five Stages of Grief: An Examination of the Kubler-Ross Model" by Christina Gregory, Psycom, psycom.net/depression.central.grief.html

"If You Are the Survivor," Social Security Administration, ssa.gov/benefits/survivors/ifyou.html

"Local and National Support," HealGrief.org, healgrief.org/grief-support-resources/

My Grief Angels, mygriefangels.org/home.html

ADDITIONAL RESOURCES FOR CHILDREN

"Affiliates and National Organizations," Children's Bereavement Center, childbereavement .org/resources/helpful-links.html

"Grief," Sesame Street for Military Families, sesamestreetformilitaryfamilies.org/topic/grief

"Helping Children Cope with Grief," Child Mind Institute, childmind.org/guide/helping -children-cope-grief/

"Helping Children Grieve" by Kathleen Smith, Psycom, psycom.net/helping-children-grieve

The National Alliance for Children's Grief promotes awareness of the needs of children and teens grieving a death and provides education and resources for anyone who wants to support them, 866-432-1542, childrengrieve.org

Uplift Center for Grieving Children provides excellent information and resources, upliftphilly .org/programs/uplift-resources/tip-sheets

Probate Laws, Codes, and Statutes

To report the death to Social Security call 1-800-722-1213.

IRS general estate information can be found online at irs.gov/businesses/small-businesses-self-employed/deceased-taxpayers-probate-filing-estate-and-individual-returns-paying-taxes-due

The following is a state-by-state reference list to codes, statutes, and laws pertaining to probate. The laws and codes of each state may change or be updated from time to time, but this should provide a starting point.

Alabama

alisondb.legislature.state.al.us/alison/CodeOfAlabama/1975/Coatoc.htm

Alaska

courts.alaska.gov/shc/probate/probate-laws.htm

Arizona

azleg.gov/arsDetail/?title=14

Arkansas

law.justia.com/codes/arkansas/2012/title-28/

California

leginfo.legislature.ca.gov/faces/codesTOCSelected.xhtml?tocCode=PROB&tocTitle=+Probate+Code+-+PROB

Colorado

statelaws.findlaw.com/colorado-law/colorado-probate-and-estate-tax-laws.html

Connecticut

cga.ct.gov/current/pub/title_45a.htm

Delaware

delcode.delaware.gov/title12/c013/index.html

District of Columbia

code.dccouncil.us/dc/council/code/titles/20/

Florida

leg.state.fl.us/statutes/index.cfm?App_mode=Display_Index&Title_Request=XLII#TitleXLII

Georgia

codes.findlaw.com/ga/title-53-wills-trusts-and-administration-of-estates/

Hawaii

law.justia.com/codes/hawaii/2013/title-30a/chapter-560/

Idaho

legislature.idaho.gov/statutesrules/idstat/title15/

Illinois

ilga.gov/legislation/ilcs/ilcs5.asp?ActID=2104&ChapterID=60

Indiana

184.175.130.101/legislative/laws/2020/ic/titles/029

Iowa
legis.iowa.gov/docs/ico/chapter/633.pdf

Kansas
ksrevisor.org/statutes/ksa_ch59.html

Kentucky
apps.legislature.ky.gov/law/statutes/chapter.aspx?id=39195

Louisiana
legis.la.gov/legis/Law.aspx?d=813956

Maine
legislature.maine.gov/statutes/18-C/title18-Cch0sec0.html

Maryland
registers.maryland.gov/main/publications/infoguide.html

Massachusetts
malegislature.gov/Laws/GeneralLaws/Partii/Titleii/Chapter190b

Michigan
legislature.mi.gov/doc.aspx?mcl-700-2519

Minnesota
www.revisor.mn.gov/statutes/cite/524

Mississippi
law.justia.com/codes/mississippi/2010/title-91/7/

Missouri
revisor.mo.gov/main/OneTitle.aspx?title=XXXI

Montana
leg.mt.gov/bills/2019/billhtml/SB0225.htm

Nebraska
nebraskalegislature.gov/laws/statutes.php?statute=30-2209

Nevada
leg.state.nv.us/nrs/nrs-136.html

New Hampshire
http://www.gencourt.state.nh.us/rsa/html/nhtoc/nhtoc-lvi.htm

New Jersey
state.nj.us/treasury/taxation/documents/pdf/guides/General-%20Guide-to-Being-an-Executor.pdf

New Mexico
nmlegis.gov/sessions/11%20regular/final/SB0146.pdf

New York
nysenate.gov/legislation/laws/EPT

North Carolina
ncleg.gov/EnactedLegislation/Statutes/PDF/ByChapter/Chapter_28A.pdf

North Dakota
legis.nd.gov/cencode/t30-1.html

Ohio
codes.ohio.gov/ohio-revised-code/title-21

Oklahoma
oksenate.gov/sites/default/files/2019-12/os58.pdf

Oregon
www.oregonlegislature.gov/bills_laws/ors/ors111.html

Pennsylvania
legis.state.pa.us/WU01/LI/LI/CT/HTM/20/20.HTM

Rhode Island
webserver.rilin.state.ri.us/Statutes/TITLE33/INDEX.HTM

South Carolina
scstatehouse.gov/code/title62.php

South Dakota
sdlegislature.gov/Statutes/Codified_Laws/2051986

Tennessee
tncourts.gov/sites/default/files/docs/probate_manual_final.pdf

Texas
statutes.capitol.texas.gov/Docs/SDocs/ESTATESCODE.pdf

Utah
le.utah.gov/xcode/Title75/75.html

Vermont
legislature.vermont.gov/statutes/title/14

Virginia
law.lis.virginia.gov/vacodefull/title64.2/chapter4/article5/

Washington
app.leg.wa.gov/rcw/default.aspx?Cite=11

West Virginia
www.wvlegislature.gov/wvcode/Code.cfm?chap=42&art=1

Wisconsin
docs.legis.wisconsin.gov/statutes/statutes/856

Wyoming
wyoleg.gov/statutes/compress/title02.pdf

Glossary of Terms

administrator: A person charged with administering the estate of a person who died without any formal estate plan. The administrator is usually defined by statute, appointed by the court, and has the authority to wrap up the affairs of a decedent.

advance directive: A legal document signed to appoint a healthcare representative and give specific instructions about healthcare, such as tube feeding and life support. (See also health-care power of attorney.)

arbitration: An alternative to court litigation. Arbitration is a means to resolve disputes in a more formal setting than mediation. An arbitrator makes decisions about the resolution of a case rather than a mediator who works to reach a settlement for the parties involved.

beneficiary: An individual or entity that receives a benefit, whether principal or income (property), from a trust. A beneficiary may also be designated on life insurance policies or other accounts such as 401(k) and IRA accounts. On these types of accounts, the beneficiary will receive the benefit directly without the necessity of probate. (See beneficiary designations.)

beneficiary accounts: Accounts that pass by operation of contract law to a designated beneficiary. Typical beneficiary accounts include life insurance contracts, IRA accounts, and 401(k) accounts.

beneficiary designations: The person or entity selected by the owner of a beneficiary account to receive the benefits of the account following the death of the account owner.

bequest: The process of making a gift of personal property in a will. (See also devise.)

codicil: A document used to change an existing will. It must be executed with the same formalities as a will in order for it to be valid.

contingent beneficiary: A secondary beneficiary to receive property by beneficiary designation when the primary beneficiary is unable or unwilling to receive benefits.

corpus property: Property held in a trust.

decedent: A person who has died.

devise: The process of making a gift of real property in a will. (See also bequest.)

devisee: The person or entity that is the recipient of a devise by will.

disclaimer: The process of refusing the benefit of a devise, bequest, or trust disposition so that the property passes to the next interest defined in the instrument or by law. A disclaimer must be made within nine months of the date of death and the person disclaiming may not accept any benefits (income or otherwise) of the property to be disclaimed. Disclaimers are used most often in postmortem planning.

donee: A person or entity receiving property, real or personal, by gift.

donor: A person making a gift. This person is responsible for any transfer tax.

estate: All the property of a decedent, including real property, personal property, and property passing by beneficiary designation.

estate tax: The federal tax on the transfer of property upon the death of an individual.

executor: The person appointed by the court as personal representative to handle the affairs of a decedent who passed away with a valid will.

fiduciary: A general term used to describe an administrator, executor, trustee, or other trusted person acting on behalf of an estate or individual.

gift tax: The federal tax imposed on the transfer of property to others during life. An exemption from tax may be available in some circumstances.

grantor: The person transferring property to a trust or making a grant of property to another.

healthcare power of attorney: A form used to appoint a person to make healthcare decisions for another who is otherwise incapacitated and unable to make decisions on their own.

heir: A person receiving property by operation of intestacy law.

inheritance: What heirs receive in an intestate estate. (See also intestacy.)

inheritance tax: The federal transfer tax at death is known as the estate tax. The state component of such tax is oftentimes referred to as an inheritance tax.

inter vivos: A Latin term meaning *during life*.

intestacy: The passing of property by state statute where there are no valid planning documents. In many jurisdictions, probate is required for an intestate estate.

joint property: Owning property with another, either with right of survivorship or as tenants in common.

letters testamentary: Documents prepared and delivered by a court to an administrator or executor giving that person the authority to act on behalf of the estate of a decedent.

living trust: A trust established during the lifetime of the trustor/grantor for purposes of avoiding probate. Most often, for simple trusts, the person creating the trust is the trustor, trustee, and beneficiary during that person's life.

mediation: A process of resolving or settling disputes without a binding decision by an arbitrator or court.

payable-on-death accounts: Accounts that pass to a selected beneficiary automatically on the death of an account owner. These accounts often act to avoid probate.

personal property: Any property other than real property.

personal representative: The person appointed by the court as executor who receives authority to act on behalf of an estate. This person is in charge of administering and working toward closure of the estate.

postmortem: A term to describe events occurring after death.

power of attorney: A document giving the named person the authority to act on behalf of the other person or entity.

probate: A formal court process following death, with the ultimate result of transferring property owned by the deceased to the living.

real property: Land and fixtures attached to land such as a house or other buildings.

residual: That portion of a trust or estate remaining following specific bequests or devises and payment of taxes, debts, and expenses.

rider: An addition to a document.

statutes: Rules created by governing bodies such as a state legislature that define the law in a particular jurisdiction.

testamentary: A term meaning *by reason of death* or *following death.*

testamentary trust: A trust created at the time of death by terms of a will or living trust.

transfer tax: A tax, either at the state or federal level, on the transfer of property during life or at death. This tax may take the form of a gift tax (during life) or an estate tax (after death).

trust: A legal entity created by a trustor to hold property, both real and personal, subject to the terms of the trust document. The trustee manages the property for the beneficiaries.

trustee: The fiduciary named by a trust document to carry out the terms of the trust. A successor trustee is an alternate trustee in the event the original trustee is no longer capable of performing the required duties.

trustor: A person who transfers property to a trust with the understanding that the trustee will manage the property according to the terms of the trust document.

will: A document to name a personal representative, nominate guardians and conservators if necessary, give instructions for estate administration, and provide for ultimate disposition of property.

Notes

END OF LIFE PLANNING/RECORD BOOK 0322

ISBN 978-1-58270-864-5 **$24.95 U.S.**/$33.95 Can.

9 781582 708645 52495

PRINTED IN CHINA